Afro-Asiatic languages

Survival Dictionaries
Set 1 of 2

by Multi Linguis

[acw] Hijazi Arabic
[arb] Standard Arabic
[ary] Moroccan Arabic
[arz] Egyptian Arabic
[mlt] Maltese

ISBN: 9798748206006

CONTENTS

GREETINGS 1
PRONUNCIATION GUIDE..2
    [ACW] HIJAZI ARABIC 2
    [ARB] STANDARD ARABIC...4
    [ARY] MOROCCAN ARABIC 6
    [ARZ] EGYPTIAN ARABIC...9
    [MLT] MALTESE 10
AFRO-ASIATIC LANGUAGES SURVIVAL DICTIONARIES (SET 1 OF 2) 12
    [ACW] HIJAZI ARABIC. SURVIVAL DICTIONARY............................12
    [ARB] STANDARD ARABIC. SURVIVAL DICTIONARY.....................20
    [ARY] MOROCCAN ARABIC. SURVIVAL DICTIONARY....................68
    [ARZ] EGYPTIAN ARABIC. SURVIVAL DICTIONARY.......................78
    [MLT] MALTESE. SURVIVAL DICTIONARY.......................................99
ABOUT THE LANGUAGES... 125
    [ACW] HIJAZI ARABIC 125
    [ARB] STANDARD ARABIC... 126
    [ARY] MOROCCAN ARABIC 127
    [ARZ] EGYPTIAN ARABIC... 128
    [MLT] MALTESE 129
ABOUT THE MULTI LINGUIS PROJECT 130
    ABOUT THE PROJECT AND OFFERED DICTIONARIES IN GENERAL ... 130
    ABOUT DESIGN OF DICTIONARIES AND ENTRIES.................................. 131
    ABOUT DIVISION OF THE DATABASE INTO LEVELS AND THEMES 132
    ABOUT TYPES AND KINDS OF THE DICTIONARIES............................. 133
    ABOUT VARIETIES OF THE ARRANGEMENT OF LEMMAS..................... 134
    ABOUT THE SOURCE, SELECTION OF LEMMAS AND PROCESSING OF
    ENTRIES.. 135
    ABOUT ERRORS AND CHANGES IN THE SOURCE 136
    ABOUT STORES, PRICES, DISCOUNTS AND PROMOTION 136
    ABOUT PLANS FOR THE FUTURE AND ADDITIONAL SERVICES......... 137
LICENSE INFORMATION 138

Multi Linguis

GREETINGS

Multi Linguis presents you a set of small survival dictionaries of the Afro-Asiatic languages.

Each of them includes up to 999 elementary words and phrases. The entries are arranged by parts of speech and then by topics, not by the alphabet.

The book is intended to help you try out these languages, spell simple broken phrases and also get some fun.

The set 1 of 2 contains Hijazi Arabic, Standard Arabic, Moroccan Arabic, Egyptian Arabic and Maltese.

The Multi Linguis Project is based on the Wiktionary corpus. The database of the Survival Dictionaries includes 999 lemmas (words and phrases), their translations into many languages, transcriptions, transliterations and grammar information.

The sets of dictionaries are designed in an original way to be convenient and efficient. All of them are available in mobile formats (epub and mobi).

Multi Linguis is presently able to publish such books for more than 200 languages. It's planned to improve them and increase their number.

IMPORTANT NOTE:
Because of the source, up to 5% of translations in this dictionary may be improper. Some expected entries have no translation so they were omitted.

PRONUNCIATION GUIDE
[ACW] HIJAZI ARABIC

Characters

◄ | ◄◄ | ◄* | *

ا | ا | ڶ | ڶ
[a:], [a], [i], Ø

ٳ | ٳ | ٮ | ٮ
[ʔ]

ٲ | ٲ | ٺ | ٺ
[ʔ]

آ | آ | ٮٵ | ٮٵ
[ʔa:]

ب | ٮ | ٮ | ب
[b]

پ | ٠ | ٠ |
[v]

ت | ٮٵ | ٮٵ | ت
[t]

ث | ٮٵ | ٮٵ | ث
[θ]

ج | ج | ج | ج
[dʒ]

ح | ح | ح | ح
[ħ]

خ | خ | خ | خ
[x]

د | د | د | د
[d]

ذ | ذ | ذ | ذ
[ð]

ر | ر | ر | ر
[r]

ز | ز | ز | ز
[z]

س | ٮٵ | ٮٵ | س
[s]

ص | ٮٵ | ٮٵ | ص
[sˤ]

ض | ٮٵ | ٮٵ | ض
[dˤ]

ط | ط | ط | ط
[tˤ]

ظ | ظ | ظ | ظ
[ðˤ]

ع | ع | ع | ع
[ʕ]

غ | غ | غ | غ
[ɣ]

ف | ٮٵ | ٮٵ | ف
[f]

ڤ | ٠ | ٠ |
[p]

ق | ٮٵ | ٮٵ | ق
[q]

2

ك | ـك | ـكـ | كـ
[k]

ل | ـل | ـلـ | لـ
[l]

م | ـم | ـمـ | مـ
[m]

ن | ـن | ـنـ | نـ
[n]

ه | ـه | ـهـ | هـ

[h]

و | ـو | ـو | و
[w], [u:], Ø

ؤ | ـؤ | ـؤ | ؤ
[ʔ]

ي | ـي | ـيـ | يـ
[j], [i:]

ئ | ـئ | ـئـ | ئـ
[ʔ]

Diacritics

‎َ‎
[a]

‎ُ‎
[u]

‎ِ‎
[i]

‎ٰ‎
[a:]

‎ﺂ‎
[ʔa:]

‎ْ‎
no-vowel marking

‎ٌ‎
+ [n] (nazalization)

‎ٍ‎
+ [n] (nazalization)

‎ً‎
+ [n] (nazalization)

‎ّ‎
geminates consonant

[ARB] STANDARD ARABIC

Characters

◄ | ◄◄ | ◄* | *

ا | ا | ـا | ـا
[a:], [a], [i], ∅

إ | ! | ـإ | ـإ
[ʔ]

أ | أ | ـأ | ـأ
[ʔ]

آ | آ | ـآ | ـآ
[ʔa:]

ب | ـب | ـبـ | بـ
[b]

پ | . | . | .
[v]

ت | ـت | ـتـ | تـ
[t]

ث | ـث | ـثـ | ثـ
[θ]

ج | ـج | ـجـ | جـ
[dʒ]

ح | ـح | ـحـ | حـ
[ħ]

خ | ـخ | ـخـ | خـ
[x]

د | ـد | ـد | د
[d]

ذ | ذ | ـذ | ـذ
[ð]

ر | ـر | ـر | ـر
[r]

ز | ـز | ـز | ـز
[z]

س | ـس | ـسـ | سـ
[s]

ص | ـص | ـصـ | صـ
[sˤ]

ض | ـض | ـضـ | ضـ
[dˤ]

ط | ـط | ـطـ | طـ
[tˤ]

ظ | ـظ | ـظـ | ظـ
[ðˤ]

ع | ـع | ـعـ | عـ
[ʕ]

غ | ـغ | ـغـ | غـ
[ɣ]

ف | ـف | ـفـ | فـ
[f]

ڤ | . | . | .
[p]

ق | ـق | ـقـ | قـ
[q]

ك | ﻚ | ﻜ | ﻛ
[k]

ه | ﻪ | ﻬ | ﻫ
[h]

ل | ﻞ | ﻠ | ﻟ
[l]

و | ﻮ | ﻮ
[w], [uː], Ø

م | ﻢ | ﻤ | ﻣ
[m]

ؤ | ﺆ | ﺆ | ﺆ
[ʔ]

ن | ﻦ | ﻨ | ﻧ
[n]

ي | ﻲ | ﻴ | ﻳ
[j], [iː]

ئ | ﺊ | ﺌ | ﺋ
[ʔ]

Diacritics

َ
[a]

ْ
no-vowel marking

ُ
[u]

ٍ
+ [n] (nazalization)

ِ
[i]

ٌ
+ [n] (nazalization)

ـٰ
[aː]

ً
+ [n] (nazalization)

ٰ
[ʔaː]

ّ
geminates consonant

5

[ARY] MOROCCAN ARABIC

Characters

◄ | ◄◄ | ◄* | *

ا | ا | ﺎ | ﺍ
[a:], [a], [i], Ø

ء | ﺀ | ﺋ | ﺋ
[ʔ]

ﺄ | ﺄ | ﺃ | ﺃ
[ʔ]

آ | آ | آ | آ
[ʔa:]

ب | ﺐ | ﺒ | ﺑ
[b]

پ | ﭗ | ﭙ | ﭙ
[v]

ت | ﺖ | ﺘ | ﺗ
[t]

ث | ﺚ | ﺜ | ﺛ
[θ]

ج | ﺞ | ﺠ | ﺟ
[dʒ]

ح | ﺢ | ﺤ | ﺣ
[ħ]

خ | ﺦ | ﺨ | ﺧ
[x]

د | ﺪ | ﺪ | ﺩ
[d]

ذ | ذ | ذ | ذ
[ð]

ر | ﺮ | ﺮ | ﺭ
[r]

ز | ﺰ | ﺰ | ﺯ
[z]

س | ﺲ | ﺴ | ﺳ
[s]

ﭺ | ﭻ | ﭼ | ﭼ
[s]

ﭖ | ﭗ | ﭙ | ﭙ
[q]

ص | ﺺ | ﺼ | ﺻ
[sˤ]

ض | ﺾ | ﻀ | ﺿ
[dˤ]

ط | ﻂ | ﻄ | ﻃ
[tˤ]

ظ | ﻆ | ﻈ | ﻇ
[ðˤ]

ع | ﻊ | ﻌ | ﻋ
[ʕ]

غ | ﻎ | ﻐ | ﻏ
[ɣ]

ڢ | ﺐ | ﺒ | ﻓ
[f]

6

ن	نـ	ـنـ	ـن
[n]

ڤ	.	.	.
[p]

ه	هـ	ـهـ	ـه
[h]

ق	.	.	.
[q]

و	و	و	و
[w], [u:], Ø

پ	.	.	.
[v]

ؤ	ؤ	ؤ	ؤ
[ʔ]

ڭ	.	.	.
[g]

ي	.	.	.
[j], [i:]

ك	ک	ک	ک
[k]

ى	ـى	ـى	ى
[j], [i:]

ل	ـل	ـلـ	لـ
[l]

ئ	ئـ	ـئـ	ـئ
[ʔ]

م	مـ	ـمـ	ـم
[m]

Diacritics

َ
[a]

ْ
no-vowel marking

ُ
[u]

ً
+ [n] (nazalization)

ِ
[i]

ٍ
+ [n] (nazalization)

ا
[a:]

ٌ
+ [n] (nazalization)

آ
[ʔa:]

ّ
geminates consonant

7

[ARZ] EGYPTIAN ARABIC

Characters

◄ | ◄◄ | ◄* | *

ا | ا | ا | ا
[a:], [a], [i], Ø

إ | إ | إ | إ
[ʔ]

أ | أ | أ | أ
[ʔ]

آ | آ | آ | آ
[ʔa:]

ب | ب | ب | ب
[b]

پ | ـ | ـ | ـ
[v]

ت | ت | ت | ت
[t]

ث | ث | ث | ث
[θ]

ج | ج | ج | ج
[dʒ]

چ | ـ | ـ | ـ
[ʒ]

ح | ح | ح | ح
[ħ]

خ | خ | خ | خ
[x]

د | د | د | د
[d]

ذ | ذ | ذ | ذ
[ð]

ر | ر | ر | ر
[r]

ز | ز | ز | ز
[z]

س | س | س | س
[s]

ص | ص | ص | ص
[sˤ]

ض | ض | ض | ض
[dˤ]

ط | ط | ط | ط
[tˤ]

ظ | ظ | ظ | ظ
[ðˤ]

ع | ع | ع | ع
[ʕ]

غ | غ | غ | غ
[ɣ]

ف | ف | ف | ف
[f]

ڤ | ـ | ـ | ـ
[p]

9

ق | ق | ـقـ | ـق
[q]

ه | ـهـ | ـه | ه
[h]

ك | كـ | ـكـ | ـك
[k]

و | و | ـو | ـو
[w], [uː], Ø

ل | لـ | ـلـ | ـل
[l]

ؤ | ؤ | ـؤ | ـؤ
[ʔ]

م | مـ | ـمـ | ـم
[m]

ي | يـ | ـيـ | ـي
[j], [iː]

ن | نـ | ـنـ | ـن
[n]

ئ | ئـ | ـئـ | ـئ
[ʔ]

Diacritics

َ
[a]

ْ
no-vowel marking

ُ
[u]

ٌ
+ [n] (nazalization)

ِ
[i]

ٍ
+ [n] (nazalization)

ٰ
[aː]

ً
+ [n] (nazalization)

ٓ
[ʔaː]

ّ
geminates consonant

9

[MLT] MALTESE

a | A
[ɐ], [aː], [æː]

b | B
[b]

ċ | Ċ
[tʃ]

d | D
[d]

e | E
[eː], [ɛ], [øː], [ə]

f | F
[f]

g | G
[g]

ġ | Ġ
[dʒ]

għ
[(ˤ)ː], [ħː]

h | H
Ø, [ħ]

ħ | Ħ
[ħ]

i | I
[iː], [iː], [ɪ]

ie
[ɛː], [iːə]

j | J
[j]

k | K
[k]

l | L
[l]

m | M
[m]

n | N
[n]

o | O
[o], [ɔ], [ɒ]

p | P
[p]

q | Q
[ʔ]

r | R
[r], [ɹ]

s | S
[s]

t | T
[t]

u | U
[u], [ʉ], [ʊ]

v | V
[v]

w | W
[w]

x | X
[ʃ], [ʒ]

z | Z
[ts], [dz]

ż | Ż
[z]

AFRO-ASIATIC LANGUAGES
SURVIVAL DICTIONARIES
(SET 1 OF 2)

[ACW] HIJAZI ARABIC. SURVIVAL DICTIONARY

corner ▪ *[012, n]*
▪ ركن ◦ <m> ▪ |rukun| ◦ /rukun/

stick ▪ *[023, n]*
▪ عَصاية ◦ <f> ▪ |'aṣāya| ◦ /ʕaˈsˤaːja/

light ▪ *[035, n]*
▪ نور ◦ <m> ▪ |nūr|

color ▪ *[036, n]*
▪ لـون ◦ <m> ▪ |lōn| ◦ /loːn/

taste ▪ *[041, n]*
▪ ذوق ◦ <m> ▪ |zōg| ◦ /zoːg/

smell ▪ *[042, n]*
▪ ريحـة ◦ <f> ▪ |rīḥa| ◦ /ˈriːħa/

fire ▪ *[046, n]*
▪ نـار ▪ |nār|

gold ▪ *[050, n]*
▪ ذَهَب ◦ <m> ▪ |dahab| ◦ /dahab/

ice ▪ *[054, n]*
▪ جليـد ◦ <m> ◦ {ice} ▪ |jalīd|
▪ ثلـج ◦ <m> ◦ {ice cubes} ▪ |talj| ◦ /ˈtald͡ʒ/

sand ▪ *[056, n]*
▪ رَمِل ◦ <m> ▪ |ramil| ◦ /ramil/

glass ▪ *[059, n]* ▪ *substance*
▪ قـزاز ◦ <m> ▪ |guzāz| ◦ /guˈzaːz/

gasoline ▪ *[065, n]*
▪ بَنْزين ▪ |banzīn| ◦ /banˈziːn/

east ▪ *[071, n]*
▪ شَرْق ◦ <m> ▪ |šarg| ◦ /ˈʃarg/

place ▪ *[075, n]*
▪ مَكان ◦ <m> ▪ |makān|

time ▪ *[076, n]* ▪ *passing of events*
▪ وَقْت ◦ <m> ▪ |wagt|

minute ▪ *[078, n]*
▪ دَقيقة ◦ <f> ▪ |dagīga|

second ▪ *[079, n]*
▪ ثانْية ◦ <f> ▪ |ṭānya|

day ▪ *[080, n]*
▪ يـوم ◦ <m> ▪ |yōm| ◦ /joːm/

week ▪ *[085, n]*

▪ أُسبوع <m> ▪ |usbū'| ▫ /ʕuːdsu/

month ▪ *[087, n]*

▪ شـهر <m> ▪ |šahar|

summer ▪ *[091, n]*

▪ صــيف <m> ▪ |ṣēf| ▫ /'sˤeːf/

wedding ▪ *[099, n]*

▪ زواج <m> ▪ |zawāj| ▫ /za'waːd͡ʒ/

chance ▪ *[101, n]*

▪ فُرْصة <f> ▪ |furṣa| ▫ /fursˤa/

star ▪ *[106, n]*

▪ نَجْمَة <f> ▪ |najma| ▫ /nad͡ʒma/

moon ▪ *[107, n]*

▪ مَرَقَ <m> ▪ |gamar|

sun ▪ *[108, n]*

▪ شَمْس <f> ▪ |šams|

cloud ▪ *[111, n]*

▪ ســحابة <f> ▪ |saḥāba|

snow ▪ *[114, n]*

▪ ثلــج <m> ▪ |talj| ▫ /'tald͡ʒ/

wind ▪ *[115, n]*

▪ ريـاح <f> ▪ |riyāḥ| ▫ /rijaːħ/

sea ▪ *[116, n]*

▪ بَحَر <m> ▪ |baḥar| ▫ /baħar/

river ▪ *[118, n]*

▪ نهر <m> ▪ |nahar|

cave ▪ *[123, n]*

▪ كَهْف <m> ▪ |kahf| ▫ /kahf/

forest ▪ *[129, n]*

▪ غابــة <f> ▪ |ḡāba| ▫ /'ɣaːba/

road ▪ *[134, n]*

▪ طَريق <m> ▪ |ṭarīg|

bridge ▪ *[137, n]*

▪ جِسِر <m> ▪ |jisir| ▫ /d͡ʒisir/

roof ▪ *[144, n]*

▪ سَطُوح <m> ▪ |saṭūḥ| ▫ /sa'tˤuːħ/

window ▪ *[149, n]*

▪ شـــباك <m> ▪ |šubbāk| ▫ /ʃuˈbːaːk/

kitchen ▪ *[153, n]*

▪ مطبـخ <m> ▪ |maṭbak̲| ▫ /matˤbax/

hotel ▪ *[156, n]*

▪ فُنْدُق <m> ▪ |fundug| ▫ /fundug/

13

mirror ▪ *[162, n]*

▪ مِرَايَة □ <f> ▪ |mirāya| □ /miˈraːja/

towel ▪ *[166, n]*

▪ مِنْشَفة □ <f> ▪ |minšafa|

pot ▪ *[168, n]*

▪ قِدِر □ <m> ▪ |gidir| □ /gadar \ gidir \ gadir/ □ {one may be incorrect}

cup ▪ *[169, n]*

▪ كَاسَة □ <m> ▪ |kāsa| □ /ˈkaːsa/

glass ▪ *[170, n]* ▪ *vessel*

▪ كَاسَة □ <f> ▪ |kāsa| □ /ˈkaːsa/

plate ▪ *[171, n]*

▪ صـحن □ <m> ▪ |ṣaħan| □ /sˤaħan/

fork ▪ *[172, n]*

▪ شـوكة □ <f> ▪ |šōka| □ /ʃoːka/

knife ▪ *[173, n]*

▪ سـكينة □ <f> ▪ |sakkīna| □ /saˈkiːna \ saˈkiːna/ □ {one may be incorrect}

spoon ▪ *[174, n]*

▪ ملعقـة □ <f> ▪ |mil 'aga| □ /milˤaga/

bottle ▪ *[176, n]*

▪ قـارورة □ <f> □ {plastic} ▪ |gārūra| □ /gaːˈruːra/
▪ قُزازة □ <f> □ {glass} ▪ |guzāza|

bag ▪ *[178, n]*

▪ شَنْطَة □ <f> ▪ |šanṭa| □ /ʃantˤa/

machine ▪ *[179, n]*

▪ مَكِيَنة □ <f> ▪ |makīna|

oven ▪ *[184, n]*

▪ فُرُن □ <m> ▪ |furun| □ /furun/

tap ▪ *[186, n]*

▪ بَزبوز □ <m> ▪ |bazbūz| □ /bazˈbuːz/

car ▪ *[196, n]*

▪ سَيَّارَة □ <f> ▪ |sayyāra|

bicycle ▪ *[198, n]*

▪ بسـكليتة □ <f> ▪ |buskulēta| □ /buskuˈleːta/

train ▪ *[199, n]*

▪ قِطَار □ <m> ▪ |giṭār| □ /giˈtˤaːr/

boat ▪ *[200, n]*

▪ قَارِب □ <m> ▪ |gārib|

driver ▪ *[203, n]*

▪ سَوَّاق □ <m> ▪ |sawwāg| □ /saˈwːaːg/

dress ▪ *[207, n]*

14

■ فُسْتَان □ <m> ▪ |fustān| □ /fusˈtaːn/

jacket ▪ *[209, n]*

■ جِكِيت □ <m> ▪ |jikēt| □ /d͡ʒaˈkeːt/

shirt ▪ *[210, n]*

■ قميـص □ <m> ▪ |gamīṣ|

shoe ▪ *[217, n]*

■ جزمة □ <f> ▪ |jazma| □ /d͡ʒazma/

scarf ▪ *[218, n]*

■ شـال □ <m> ▪ |šāl| □ /ʃaːl/

umbrella ▪ *[219, n]*

■ شمسـية □ <f> ▪ |šamsiyya| □ /ʃamsijːa/

cat ▪ *[228, n]*

■ بسـة □ <f> ▪ |bissa| □ /bisːa/

chicken ▪ *[242, n]*

■ دجاجة □ <f> ▪ |dujāja| □ /duˈd͡ʒaːd͡ʒa/

back ▪ *[248, n]* ▪ *of body*

■ ظَهَر □ <m> ▪ |ḍahar| □ /dˤuhur \ dˤahar/ □ {one may be incorrect}

arm ▪ *[255, n]*

■ ذُراع □ <f> ▪ |durāʿ|

finger ▪ *[256, n]*

■ أُصْباع □ <m> ▪ |ˈuṣbā ʾ| □ /ʔuṣˤˈbaːʕ/

heart ▪ *[259, n]*

■ قلـب □ <m> ▪ |galb| □ /ˈgalb/

face ▪ *[274, n]*

■ وَجْه □ <m> ▪ |wajh|

eye ▪ *[275, n]*

■ عيـن □ <f> ▪ |ʿēn|

nose ▪ *[277, n]*

■ خشـم □ <m> ▪ |ḵušum| □ /xuʃum/

food ▪ *[280, n]*

■ أَكِل □ <m> ▪ |ʾakil|

lunch ▪ *[282, n]*

■ غدا □ <m> ▪ |ḡada| □ /ɣada/

bread ▪ *[296, n]*

■ بـزخُ □ <m> ▪ |ḵubuz| □ /xubuz/

cheese ▪ *[297, n]*

■ جبنـة □ <f> ▪ |jubna| □ /d͡ʒubna/

chocolate ▪ *[303, n]*

■ شُكَلاطة □ <f> ▪ |šukalāṭa| □ /ʃukaˈlaːtˤa/

spice ▪ *[306, n]*

■ بَهَار □ <m> ▪ |bahār|

coffee • *[308, n]*

▪ قَهْوَة □ <f> ▪ |gahwa| □ /ˈgah.wa/

tea • *[309, n]*

▪ شاهي □ <m> ▪ |šāhi| □ /ˈʃaːhi/

wine • *[311, n]*

▪ خَمُر □ <m> ▪ |ḵamur| □ /xamur/

restaurant • *[312, n]*

▪ مَطْعَم □ <m> ▪ |maṭ 'am|

dream • *[313, n]*

▪ حلم □ <m> ▪ |ḥilim|

mind • *[318, n]*

▪ عَقِل □ <m> ▪ |ˈagil|

book • *[328, n]*

▪ كتــاب □ <m> ▪ |kitāb| □ /kiˈtaːb/

pen • *[333, n]*

▪ قلـم □ <m> ▪ |galam| □ /galam/

name • *[337, n]*

▪ اسـم □ <m> ▪ |isim| □ /isim/

word • *[338, n]*

▪ كلمـة □ <f> ▪ |kilma| □ /kilma/

language • *[340, n]*

▪ لُغَة □ <f> ▪ |luḡa|

message • *[346, n]*

▪ رسالة ▪ |risāla| □ /riˈsaːla/

story • *[347, n]*

▪ قصـة □ <f> ▪ |giṣṣa| □ /gisˤːa \ gasˤːa/ □ {one may be incorrect}

culture • *[349, n]*

▪ ثقافـة □ <f> ▪ |ṯaqāfa| □ /saˈgaːfa/ □ {speakers with full /θ/ and /s/ merger}

man • *[355, n]*

▪ رِجَّال □ <m> ▪ |rijjāl| □ /riˈd͡ʒːaːl/

wife • *[359, n]*

▪ زُوجَة □ <f> ▪ |zōja|

family • *[360, n]*

▪ عيلــة □ <f> ▪ |ˈēla| □ /ˈʕeːla/

sister • *[366, n]*

▪ أخت □ <f> ▪ |ˈuḵt| □ /ˈʔuxt/

music • *[381, n]*

▪ مُسيقى □ <f> ▪ |musīga|

song • *[382, n]*

▪ أُغْنِيَة □ <f> ▪ |uḡniya| □ /ʔuɣnija/

16

guitar ▪ *[383, n]*

▪ قيتــــار □ <m> ▪ | gītār | □ /giːˈtaːr/

coin ▪ *[402, n]*

▪ قِرْش □ <m> ▪ | girš | □ /girʃ/

shop ▪ *[410, n]*

▪ مَحَل □ <m> ▪ | maḥal | □ /ˈmaħalː/

tool ▪ *[417, n]*

▪ عِدَّة □ <f pl> ▪ | ʕidda |

scissors ▪ *[418, n]*

▪ مَقَص □ <m> ▪ | magaṣ | □ /magasʕːː/

king ▪ *[434, n]*

▪ مَلِك □ <m> ▪ | malik |

army ▪ *[435, n]*

▪ جيــش □ <m> ▪ | jēš | □ /ˈd͡ʒeːʃ/

sword ▪ *[440, n]*

▪ ســيف □ <m> ▪ | sēf |

bomb ▪ *[442, n]*

▪ قُنْبُلة □ <f> ▪ | gunbula | □ /gunbula/

close ▪ *[472, v]*

▪ سَكَّر ▪ | sakkar |

measure ▪ *[473, v]*

▪ قــاس ▪ | gās |

go ▪ *[483, v]*

▪ راح ▪ | rāḥ |

come ▪ *[489, v]*

▪ جا ▪ | jā |

walk ▪ *[491, v]*

▪ مِشِي ▪ | miši |

run ▪ *[492, v]*

▪ جري ▪ | jiri |

jump ▪ *[497, v]*

▪ نـط ▪ | naṭṭ | □ /ˈnatʕːː/

drink ▪ *[552, v]*

▪ شِرِب ▪ | širib |

read ▪ *[584, v]*

▪ قَرَا ▪ | gara |

cry ▪ *[593, v]*

▪ بِكِي ▪ | biki |

miss ▪ *[596, v]*

▪ أَوْحَشْ ▪ | ˈawḥaš | □ /ʔawħaʃ/

want ▪ *[598, v]*

▪ بِغِي ▪ | biḡi |

17

say ▪ *[608, v]*

▪ يِقول ▪ |yigūl|

talk ▪ *[615, v]*

▪ بِتْكَلَّم ▪ |yitkallam|

empty ▪ *[660, adj]*

▪ فاضـي ▪ |fāḍi|

thick ▪ *[672, adj]*

▪ سَميك ▪ |samīk|

blue ▪ *[681, adj]*

▪ أزرق ▪ |azrag| ▫ /ʔazrag/

fake ▪ *[748, adj]*

▪ تَقْليد ▪ |taglīd| ▫ /tagˈliːd/

angry ▪ *[784, adj]*

▪ مُعَصِّب <m> ▪ ▫ |mu ˈaṣṣib| ▫ /muˈʕaˈsˤːib/

also ▪ *[808, adv]*

▪ كَمَان ▪ |kamān| ▫ /kaˈmaːn/

here ▪ *[823, adv]*

▪ هنا ▪ |hina|

now ▪ *[831, adv]*

▪ دحيـن ▪ |daḥēn, daḥīn| ▫ /daˈħeːn/

already ▪ *[845, adv]*

▪ قِد ▪ |gid|

maybe ▪ *[848, adv]*

▪ يمكـن ▪ |yimkin| ▫ /jimkinː/

she ▪ *[855, prn]*

▪ هي ▪ |hiyya|

nothing ▪ *[871, prn]*

▪ شـي ولا ▪ |wala šay|

what ▪ *[873, prn]*

▪ إيـش ▪ |ˈēš| ▫ /ʔeːʃ/

that ▪ *[876, det]*

▪ ذاك <m> ▫ ▪ |dāk|

no ▪ *[878, det]*

▪ مـافي ▪ |māfi|

zero ▪ *[899, num]*

▪ صـفر <m> ▫ ▪ |ṣifir|

one ▪ *[900, num]*

▪ واحد <m> ▫ ▪ |wāḥid|

million ▪ *[919, num]*

▪ مِلْيون <m> ▫ ▪ |milyōn| ▫ /milˈjoːn/

and ▪ *[925, cnj]* ▪ *similar words*

▪ و ▪ |u| ▫ /u/

18

until ▪ *[980, prp]*

    ▪ إليـــن ▪ |ˈilēn| ▫ /ʔileːn/

please ▪ *[989, int]*

    ▪ سَمَحْت لَو ▫ {to a male} ▪ |law samaḥt| ▫ /law samaħt/

    ▪ سَمَحْتي لَو ▫ {to a female} ▪ |law samaḥti| ▫ /law samaħt/

yes ▪ *[996, int]*

    ▪ إيـوه ▪ |īwa| ▫ /ʔiːwa/ ▫ {of adverb}

no ▪ *[997, int]*

    ▪ لَأ ▪ |laʾ|

[ARB] STANDARD ARABIC. SURVIVAL DICTIONARY

thing ▪ *[001, n]*
　　　　　　　▪ □ شَيْء □ <m> ▪ |šay'|

amount ▪ *[002, n]*
　　　　　　　▪ □ مَبْلَغ □ <m> ▪ |mablaḡ|

part ▪ *[003, n]*
　　　　　　　▪ □ جُزْء □ <m> ▪ |juz'| □ /d͡ʒuzʔ/

half ▪ *[004, n]*
　　　　　　　▪ □ نِصْف □ <m> ▪ |niṣf|

quarter ▪ *[005, n]*
　　　　　　　▪ □ رُبْع □ <m> ▪ |rub'|

group ▪ *[006, n]*
　　　　　　　▪ □ مَجْمُوعَة □ <f> ▪ |majmū'a|

pair ▪ *[007, n]*
　　　　　　　▪ □ زَوْج □ <m> ▪ |zawj| □ /zawd͡ʒ/

member ▪ *[008, n]*
　　　　　　　▪ □ عُضُو □ <m> ▪ |'uḍū|

cross ▪ *[009, n]*
　　　　　　　▪ □ صَلِيب □ <m> ▪ |ṣalīb|

line ▪ *[010, n]*
　　　　　　　▪ □ خَطّ ▪ |ḵaṭṭ|

shape ▪ *[011, n]*
　　　　　　　▪ □ شَكْل □ <m> ▪ |šakl|

corner ▪ *[012, n]*
　　　　　　　▪ □ زَاوِيَة □ <f> ▪ |zāwiya|

side ▪ *[013, n]*
　　　　　　　▪ □ جَانِب □ <m> ▪ |jānib|

bottom ▪ *[014, n]*
　　　　　　　▪ □ قَاع □ <m> ▪ |qā'|

top ▪ *[015, n]*
　　　　　　　▪ □ قِمَّة □ <f> ▪ |qimma| □ /qim.ma/

front ▪ *[016, n]*
　　　　　　　▪ □ أَمَام □ <m> ▪ |'amām|

middle ▪ *[018, n]*
　　　　　　　▪ □ مُنْتَصَف □ <m> ▪ |muntaṣaf| □ /mun.ta.sˤaf/

hole ▪ *[019, n]*
　　　　　　　▪ □ حُفْرَة □ <f> ▪ |ḥufra|

circle ▪ *[020, n]*
　　　　　　　▪ □ دَائِرَة □ <f> ▪ |dā'ira| □ /daː.ʔi.rah/

square ▪ *[021, n]* ▪ *polygon*
　　　　　　　▪ □ مُرَبَّع □ <m> ▪ |murabba'|

triangle • *[022, n]*

■ مُثَلَّث ◌ <m> ■ | muṯallaṯ | ◌ /mu.θal.laθ/

stick • *[023, n]*

■ عَصًا ◌ <m> ■ | ʾaṣan | ◌ /ʕa.sˤan/

sheet • *[024, n]*

■ وَرَقَة ◌ <f> ■ | waraqa |

chain • *[025, n]*

■ سِلْسِلَة ◌ <f> ■ | silsila | ◌ /sil.si.la/

rope • *[026, n]*

■ حَبْل ◌ <m> ■ | ḥabl |

pipe • *[027, n]*

■ مَاسُورَة ◌ <f> ■ | māsūra | ◌ /maː.suː.ra/

size • *[028, n]*

■ مَقَاس ◌ <m> ■ | maqās |

metre • *[030, n]*

■ مِتْر ◌ <m> ■ | mitr |

ruler • *[031, n]*

■ مِسْطَرَة ◌ <f> ■ | misṭara | ◌ /mis.tˤa.ra/

litre • *[032, n]*

■ لِتْر ◌ <m> ■ | litr |

weight • *[033, n]*

■ وَزْن ■ | wazn |

kilogram • *[034, n]*

■ كِيلُوغْرَام ◌ <m> ■ | kīlūḡrām | ◌ /kiː.luɣ.raːm/

light • *[035, n]*

■ نُور ◌ <m> ■ | nūr | ◌ /naw.wa.ra/

color • *[036, n]*

■ لَوْن ◌ <m> ■ | lawn | ◌ /lawn/

sound • *[037, n]*

■ صَوْت ◌ <m> ■ | ṣawt |

noise • *[038, n]*

■ ضَوْضَاء ◌ <m> ■ | ḍawḍāʾ |

temperature • *[039, n]*

■ دَرَجَة أَلْحَرَارَة ◌ <f> ■ | darajat al-ḥarāra | ◌ /da.ra.dʒat al.ħa.raː.ra/

degree • *[040, n]*

■ دَرَجَة ◌ <f> ■ | daraja | ◌ /da.ra.dʒa/

taste • *[041, n]*

■ ذَوْق ■ | ḍawq |

smell • *[042, n]*

■ رَائِحَة ◌ <f> ■ | rāʾiḥa | ◌ /raː.ʔi.ħa/

gas • *[043, n]*

21

liquid ▪ *[044, n]*

▪ غَاز ▫ <m> ▪ |ḡāz| ▫ /ɣaːz/

dust ▪ *[045, n]*

▪ سَائِل ▫ <m> ▪ |sāʾil|

fire ▪ *[046, n]*

▪ غُبَار ▫ <m> ▪ |ḡubār| ▫ /ɣu.baːr/

smoke ▪ *[047, n]*

▪ نَار ▫ <f> ▪ |nār| ▫ /naːr/

match ▪ *[048, n]*

▪ دُخَان ▫ <m> ▪ |duk̲ān|

metal ▪ *[049, n]*

▪ ثِقَاب عُود ▫ <m> ▪ |ʿūd t̲iqāb|

gold ▪ *[050, n]*

▪ مَعْدَن ▫ <m> ▪ |maʿdan|

iron ▪ *[051, n]*

▪ ذَهَب ▫ <m/f> ▪ |d̲ahab| ▫ /ða.ha.ba/ ▫ {of verb}

silver ▪ *[052, n]*

▪ حَدِيد ▫ <m> ▪ |ḥadīd|

water ▪ *[053, n]*

▪ فِضَّة ▫ <f> ▪ |fiḍḍa| ▫ /ˈfidˤːa/

ice ▪ *[054, n]*

▪ مَاء ▪ |māʾ| ▫ /maːʔ/

air ▪ *[055, n]*

▪ جَلِيد ▫ <m> ▪ |jalīd|

sand ▪ *[056, n]*

▪ هَوَاء ▫ <m> ▪ |hawāʾ| ▫ /ha.waːʔ/

stone ▪ *[057, n]*

▪ رَمْل ▫ <m> ▪ |raml| ▫ /raml/

earth ▪ *[058, n]*

▪ حَجَر ▫ <m> ▪ |ḥajar|

glass ▪ *[059, n]* ▪ substance

▪ تُرْبَة ▫ <f> ▪ |turba| ▫ /tur.ba/

paint ▪ *[060, n]*

▪ زُجَاج ▫ <m> ▪ |zujāj|

wood ▪ *[061, n]*

▪ دِهَان ▫ <m> ▪ |dihān|

paper ▪ *[062, n]*

▪ خَشَب ▫ <m> ▪ |k̲ašab|

leather ▪ *[064, n]*

▪ وَرَق ▫ <f> ▪ |waraq| ▫ /wa.raq/

gasoline ▪ *[065, n]*

▪ جِلْد ▫ <m> ▪ |jild|

▪ بَنْزِين ◦ <m> ▪ |banzīn|

soap ▪ [067, n]

▪ صَابُون ◦ <m> ▪ |ṣābūn|

distance ▪ [068, n]

▪ مَسَافَة ◦ <f> ▪ |masāfa|

step ▪ [069, n]

▪ خُطْوَة ◦ <f> ▪ |ḵuṭwa|

direction ▪ [070, n]

▪ إتِّجَاه ◦ <m> ▪ |ittijāh|

east ▪ [071, n]

▪ شَرْق ◦ <m> ▪ |šarq| ◦ /ʃarq/

north ▪ [072, n]

▪ شَمَال ◦ <m> ▪ |šamāl| ◦ /ʃi.maːl \ ʃa.maːl/ ◦ {one may be incorrect}

south ▪ [073, n]

▪ جَنُوب ◦ <m> ▪ |janūb| ◦ /d͡ʒa.nuːb/

west ▪ [074, n]

▪ غَرْب ◦ <m> ▪ |ḡarb|

place ▪ [075, n]

▪ مَكَان ◦ <m> ▪ |makān| ◦ /ma.kaːn/

time ▪ [076, n] ▪ passing of events

▪ زَمَن ◦ <m> ▪ |zaman| ◦ /za.man/

hour ▪ [077, n]

▪ سَاعَة ◦ <f> ▪ |sāʿa| ◦ /saː.ʕa/

minute ▪ [078, n]

▪ دَقِيقَة ◦ <f> ▪ |daqīqa| ◦ /da.qiː.qa/

second ▪ [079, n]

▪ ثَانِيَة ◦ <f> ▪ |ṯāniya| ◦ /ˈθaːnjə/ ◦ {Gulf Arabic}

day ▪ [080, n]

▪ يَوْم ◦ <m> ▪ |yawm| ◦ /jawm/

afternoon ▪ [081, n]

▪ الزَّوَال بَعْدَ ▪ |baʿda z-zawāl|

evening ▪ [082, n]

▪ مَسَاء ◦ <m> ▪ |masāʾ|

morning ▪ [083, n]

▪ صَبَاح ◦ <m> ▪ |ṣabāḥ|

night ▪ [084, n]

▪ لَيْلَة ◦ <f sgv> ▪ |layla| ◦ /laj.la/
▪ لَيْل ◦ <col> ▪ |layl| ◦ /lajl/

week ▪ [085, n]

▪ أُسْبُوع ◦ <m> ▪ |ʾusbūʿ|

year ▪ [086, n]

23

• عَام • | ʿām | □ /ʕaːm/

month • [087, n]

شَهْر • <m> □ | šahr | □ /ʃahr/

season • [088, n]

فَصْل • | faṣl |

autumn • [089, n]

خَرِيف • <m> □ | ḵarīf |

spring • [090, n]

رَبِيع • <m> □ | rabīʿ |

summer • [091, n]

صَيْف • <m> □ | ṣayf | □ /sˁɑif/

winter • [092, n]

شِتَاء • <m> □ | šitāʾ |

century • [093, n]

قَرْن • <m> □ | qarn | □ /qarn/

age • [094, n]

عُمْر • <m> □ | ʿumr |

history • [095, n]

تَارِيخ • <m> □ | tārīḵ | □ /taː.riːx/

event • [096, n]

وَاقِعَة • <f> □ | wāqiʿa |

holiday • [097, n]

عِيد • <m> □ | ʿīd | □ /ʕiːd/

birthday • [098, n]

مِيلَادٍ عِيدُ • <m> □ | ʿīdu mīlādin |

wedding • [099, n]

عُرْس • <m> □ | ʿurs |

time • [100, n] • instance

مَرَّة • <f> □ | marra | □ /mar.ra/

chance • [101, n]

فُرْصَة • <f> □ | furṣa |

beginning • [102, n]

بِدَايَة • <f> □ | bidāya |

end • [103, n]

نِهَايَة • <f> □ | nihāya |

clock • [104, n]

سَاعَة • <f> □ | sāʿa | □ /saː.ʕa/

space • [105, n]

فَضَاء • <m> □ | faḍāʾ | □ /fa.dˤaːʔ/

star • [106, n]

نَجْم • <m> □ | najm |

moon • [107, n]

24

sun ▪ *[108, n]*

▪ قَمَر ▫ <m> ▪ | qamar |

sky ▪ *[109, n]*

▪ شَمْس ▫ <f> ▪ | šams | ▫ /ʃams/

weather ▪ *[110, n]*

▪ سَمَاء ▫ <m/f> ▪ | samā' | ▫ /sa.maːʔ/

cloud ▪ *[111, n]*

▪ طَقْس ▫ <m> ▪ | ṭaqs | ▫ /tˤaqs/

fog ▪ *[112, n]*

▪ سَحَابَة ▫ <f> ▪ | saḥāba |

rain ▪ *[113, n]*

▪ ضَبَاب ▫ <m> ▪ | ḍabāb | ▫ /dˤi.baːb/

snow ▪ *[114, n]*

▪ مَطَر ▫ <m> ▪ | maṭar |

wind ▪ *[115, n]*

▪ ثَلْج ▫ <m> ▪ | t̲alj |

sea ▪ *[116, n]*

▪ رِيح ▫ <f> ▪ | rīḥ | ▫ /riː.ħa/ ▫ {of verb}

lake ▪ *[117, n]*

▪ بَحْر ▫ <m> ▪ | baḥr | ▫ /baħr/

river ▪ *[118, n]*

▪ بُحَيْرَة ▫ <f> ▪ | buḥayra | ▫ /bu.ħaj.ra/

wave ▪ *[119, n]*

▪ نَهْر ▫ <m> ▪ | nahr | ▫ /nahr/

coast ▪ *[120, n]*

▪ مَوْج ▫ <m> ▪ | mawj |

hill ▪ *[121, n]*

▪ سَاحِل ▪ | sāḥil |

mountain ▪ *[122, n]*

▪ تَلّ ▫ <m> ▪ | tall | ▫ /tall/

cave ▪ *[123, n]*

▪ جَبَل ▫ <m> ▪ | jabal |

world ▪ *[124, n]*

▪ كَهْف ▫ <m> ▪ | kahf |

country ▪ *[125, n]*

▪ عَالَم ▫ <m> ▪ | ʿālam |

border ▪ *[126, n]*

▪ بَلَد ▫ <f> ▪ | balad |

▪ حُدُود ▫ <n pl> ▫ {normally used in the plural} ▪ | ḥudūd |

island ▪ *[127, n]*

▪ جَزِيرَة ▫ <f> ▪ | jazīra | ▫ /dʒa.ziː.ra/

desert ▪ [128, n]

▪ صَحْرَاء <f> ▪ |ṣaḥrāʾ| ▫ /sˤaħ.raːʔ/

forest ▪ [129, n]

▪ غَابَة <f> ▪ |ḡāba| ▫ /ɣaː.ba/

city ▪ [130, n]

▪ مَدِينَة <f> ▪ |madīna| ▫ /ma.diː.na/

town ▪ [131, n]

▪ مَدِينَة <f> ▪ |madīna| ▫ /ma.diː.na/

village ▪ [132, n]

▪ قَرْيَة <f> ▪ |qarya| ▫ /qar.ja/

park ▪ [133, n]

▪ حَدِيقَة <f> ▪ |ḥadīqa| ▫ /ħa.diː.qa/

road ▪ [134, n]

▪ طَرِيق <m/f> ▪ |ṭarīq| ▫ /tˤa.riːq/

street ▪ [135, n]

▪ شَارِع <m> ▪ |šāriʿ| ▫ /ʃaː.riʕ/

square ▪ [136, n] ▪ place in town

▪ مَيْدَان <m> ▪ |maydān| ▫ /maj.daːn/

bridge ▪ [137, n]

▪ جِسْر <m> ▪ |jisr|

railway ▪ [138, n]

▪ سِكَّة حَدِيدِيَّة <f> ▪ |sikka ḥadīdiyya|

building ▪ [139, n]

▪ مَبْنَى <m> ▪ |mabnā|

house ▪ [140, n]

▪ بَيْت <m> ▪ |bayt| ▫ /bajt/

station ▪ [141, n]

▪ مَحَطَّة <f> ▪ |maḥaṭṭa| ▫ /ma.ħatˤ.tˤa/

airport ▪ [142, n]

▪ مَطَار <m> ▪ |maṭār| ▫ /ma.tˤaːr/

port ▪ [143, n]

▪ مِينَاء <m> ▪ |mīnāʾ| ▫ /miː.naːʔ/

roof ▪ [144, n]

▪ سَقْف <m> ▪ |saqf| ▫ /saqf/

wall ▪ [145, n]

▪ جِدَار <m> ▪ |jidār|

floor ▪ [146, n]

▪ أَرْضِيَّة <f> ▪ |ʾarḍiyya|

ceiling ▪ [147, n]

▪ سَقْف <m> ▪ |saqf| ▫ /saqf/

door ▪ [148, n]

▪ بَاب <m> ▪ |bāb| ▫ /baːb/

window • *[149, n]*
- نَافِذَة ◻ <f> • | nāfiḏa | ◻ /naː.fi.ða/

stairs • *[150, n]*
- سَلَالِم ◻ <m pl> • | salālim |

room • *[151, n]*
- غُرْفَة ◻ <f> • | ḡurfa | ◻ /ɣur.fa/

bathroom • *[152, n]*
- حَمَّام ◻ <m> • | ḥammām | ◻ /ħam.maːm \ ħa.maːm \ ħi.maːm/ ◻ {one may be incorrect}

kitchen • *[153, n]*
- مَطْبَخ ◻ <m> • | maṭbaḵ | ◻ /matˤ.bax/

office • *[154, n]*
- مَكْتَب ◻ <m> • | maktab | ◻ /mak.tab/

home • *[155, n]*
- بَيْت ◻ <m> • | bayt | ◻ /bajt/

hotel • *[156, n]*
- فُنْدُق ◻ <m> • | funduq | ◻ /fun.duq/

chair • *[157, n]*
- كُرْسِيّ ◻ <m> • | kursiyy | ◻ /kur.sijj/

bed • *[158, n]*
- سَرِير ◻ <m> • | sarīr |

wardrobe • *[159, n]*
- خِزَانَة ◻ <f> • | ḵizāna | ◻ /xi.zaː.na/

table • *[160, n]*
- طَاوِلَة ◻ <f> • | ṭāwila | ◻ /tˤaː.wi.la/

shelf • *[161, n]*
- رَفّ ◻ <m> • | raff | ◻ /raff/

mirror • *[162, n]*
- مِرْآة ◻ <f> • | mir'āh | ◻ /mir.ʔaːh/

carpet • *[163, n]*
- سَجَّادَة ◻ <f> • | sajjāda | ◻ /sad͡ʒ.d͡ʒaː.da/

blanket • *[164, n]*
- لِحَاف ◻ <m> • | liḥāf |

pillow • *[165, n]*
- وِسَادَة ◻ <f> • | wisāda |

towel • *[166, n]*
- مَنْشَفَة ◻ <f> • | manšafa |

curtain • *[167, n]*
- سِتَارَة ◻ <f> • | sitāra | ◻ /si.taː.ra/

pot • *[168, n]*
- قِدْر ◻ <m> • | qidr |

cup • *[169, n]*

كَأْس ◻ <m> ▪ |ka's| ◻ /kaʔs/

glass ▪ *[170, n]* ▪ *vessel*

▪ كَأْس ◻ <m> ▪ |ka's| ◻ /kaʔs/

plate ▪ *[171, n]*

▪ طَبَق ◻ <m> ▪ |ṭabaq|

fork ▪ *[172, n]*

▪ شَوْكَة ◻ <f> ▪ |šawka|

knife ▪ *[173, n]*

▪ سِكِّين ◻ <m/f> ▪ |sikkīn| ◻ /sik.kiːn/

spoon ▪ *[174, n]*

▪ مِلْعَقَة ◻ <f> ▪ |mil'aqa| ◻ /mil.ʕa.qa/

basket ▪ *[175, n]*

▪ سَلَّة ◻ <f> ▪ |salla| ◻ /sal.la/

bottle ▪ *[176, n]*

▪ زُجَاجَة ◻ <f> ▪ |zujāja| ◻ /zu.d͡ʒaː.d͡ʒa/

box ▪ *[177, n]*

▪ صُنْدُوق ◻ <m> ▪ |ṣundūq| ◻ /sˤun.duːq/

bag ▪ *[178, n]*

▪ حَقِيبَة ◻ <f> ▪ |ḥaqība|

machine ▪ *[179, n]*

▪ آلَة ◻ <f> ▪ |'āla| ◻ /ʔaːla/

battery ▪ *[180, n]*

▪ بَطَّارِيَّة ◻ <f> ▪ |baṭṭāriyya|

engine ▪ *[181, n]*

▪ مُحَرِّك ◻ <m> ▪ |muḥarrik|

button ▪ *[182, n]*

▪ زِرّ ◻ <m> ▪ |zirr|

refrigerator ▪ *[183, n]*

▪ ثَلَّاجَة ▪ |ṯallāja|

oven ▪ *[184, n]*

▪ فُرْن ◻ <m> ▪ |furn| ◻ /furn/

lamp ▪ *[185, n]*

▪ مِصْبَاح ◻ <m> ▪ |miṣbāḥ| ◻ /misˤ.baːħ/

tap ▪ *[186, n]*

▪ صُنْبُور ◻ <m> ▪ |ṣunbūr| ◻ /sˤun.buːr/

shower ▪ *[187, n]*

▪ دُش ◻ <m> ▪ |duš|

television ▪ *[189, n]* ▪ *device*

▪ تِلْفَاز ◻ <m> ▪ |tilfāz|

camera ▪ *[190, n]*

▪ كَامِيرَا ◻ <f> ▪ |kāmērā|

telephone ▪ *[191, n]*

▪ تِلِفُون ▫ <m> ▪ | tilifūn | ▫ /ti.li.fuːn/

computer ▪ *[192, n]*

▪ حَاسُوب ▫ <m> ▪ | ḥāsūb | ▫ /ħaː.suːb/

file ▪ *[193, n]*

▪ مِلَفّ ▫ <m> ▪ | milaff |

Internet ▪ *[194, n]*

▪ إِنْتِرْنِت ▫ <m> ▪ | ʾinternet |

bus ▪ *[195, n]*

▪ حَافِلَة ▫ <f> ▪ | ḥāfila | ▫ /ħaː.fi.la/

car ▪ *[196, n]*

▪ سَيَّارَة ▫ <f> ▪ | sayyāra | ▫ /saj.jaː.ra/

truck ▪ *[197, n]*

▪ شَاحِنَة ▫ <f> ▪ | šāḥina |

bicycle ▪ *[198, n]*

▪ دَرَّاجَة ▫ <f> ▪ | darrāja | ▫ /dar.raː.d͡ʒa/

train ▪ *[199, n]*

▪ قِطَار ▫ <m> ▪ | qiṭār | ▫ /qi.tˤaːr/

boat ▪ *[200, n]*

▪ قَارِب ▫ <m> ▪ | qārib | ▫ /qaː.rib/

ship ▪ *[201, n]*

▪ سَفِينَة ▫ <f> ▪ | safīna | ▫ /sa.fiː.na/

airplane ▪ *[202, n]*

▪ طَائِرَة ▫ <f> ▪ | ṭāʾira | ▫ /tˤaː.ʔi.ra/

driver ▪ *[203, n]*

▪ سَائِق ▫ <m> ▪ | sāʾiq |

passenger ▪ *[204, n]*

▪ مُسَافِر ▫ <m> ▪ | musāfir |

ticket ▪ *[205, n]*

▪ تَذْكِرَة ▫ <f> ▪ | taḏkira |

coat ▪ *[206, n]*

▪ مِعْطَف ▫ <m> ▪ | miʿṭaf | ▫ /miʕ.tˤaf/

dress ▪ *[207, n]*

▪ ثَوْب ▫ <m> ▪ | ṯawb |

suit ▪ *[208, n]*

▪ بَذْلَة ▫ <f> ▪ | baḏla | ▫ /bað.la/

jacket ▪ *[209, n]*

▪ جَاكِيت ▫ <m> ▪ | jākēt |

shirt ▪ *[210, n]*

▪ قَمِيص ▫ <m> ▪ | qamīṣ |

sweater ▪ *[211, n]*

▪ سْوِيتَر ▫ <m> ▪ | swītar |

pants ▪ *[212, n]*

29

skirt ▪ *[213, n]*

▪ بِنْطَال ▫ <m> ▪ |binṭāl|

pocket ▪ *[214, n]*

▪ تَنُّورَة ▫ <f> ▪ |tannūra|

hat ▪ *[215, n]*

▪ جَيْب ▫ <m> ▪ |jayb|

boot ▪ *[216, n]*

▪ قُبَّعَة ▫ <f> ▪ |qubbaʻa| ▫ /aʕ.ad.qub./

shoe ▪ *[217, n]*

▪ جَزْمَة ▫ <f> ▪ |jazma|

scarf ▪ *[218, n]*

▪ حِذَاء ▫ <m> ▪ |ḥiḏā'|

umbrella ▪ *[219, n]*

▪ وِشَاح ▫ <m> ▪ |wišāḥ|

ring ▪ *[220, n]*

▪ مِظَلَّة ▫ <f> ▫ {for rain} ▪ |miẓalla| ▫ /ma.ðˤal.la/
▪ شَمْسِيَّة ▫ <f> ▫ {for sun} ▪ |šamsiyya|

nature ▪ *[221, n]*

▪ خَاتَم ▫ <m> ▪ |ḵātam|

mushroom ▪ *[222, n]*

▪ طَبِيعَة ▫ <f> ▪ |ṭabīʻa|

grass ▪ *[223, n]*

▪ فُطْر ▫ <m> ▪ |fuṭr|

tree ▪ *[224, n]*

▪ حَشِيش ▫ <m> ▪ |ḥašīš| ▫ /ħa.ʃiːʃ/

leaf ▪ *[225, n]*

▪ شَجَر ▫ <m col> ▪ |šajar|
▪ شَجَرَة ▫ <f sgv> ▪ |šajara| ▫ /ʃa.d͡ʒa.ra/

flower ▪ *[226, n]*

▪ وَرَقَة ▫ <f> ▪ |waraqa|

animal ▪ *[227, n]*

▪ زَهْرَة ▫ <f> ▪ |zahra| ▫ /zah.ra/

cat ▪ *[228, n]*

▪ حَيَوَان ▫ <m> ▪ |ḥayawān| ▫ /ħa.ja.waːn/

dog ▪ *[229, n]*

▪ قِطّ ▫ <m> ▪ |qiṭṭ|

horse ▪ *[230, n]*

▪ كَلْب ▫ <m> ▪ |kalb| ▫ /kalb/

sheep ▪ *[231, n]*

▪ حِصَان ▫ <m> ▪ |ḥiṣān| ▫ /ħi.sˤaːn/

pig ▪ *[232, n]*

▪ خَرُوف ▫ <m> ▫ {both ram and sheep} ▪ |ḵarūf|

30

■ خِنْزِير □ <m> ■ |ḵinzīr| □ /xin.ziːr/

cow ▪ *[233, n]*

■ بَقَرَة □ <f> ■ |baqara| □ /ba.qa.ra/

lion ▪ *[234, n]*

■ أَسَد □ <m> ■ |ʾasad|

bear ▪ *[235, n]*

■ دُبّ □ <m> ■ |dubb| □ /dab.ba/ □ {of verb}

elephant ▪ *[236, n]*

■ فِيل □ <m> ■ |fīl| □ /fiːl/

mouse ▪ *[237, n]*

■ فَأْرَة □ <f> ■ |faʾra|

monkey ▪ *[238, n]*

■ قِرْد □ <m> ■ |qird|

snake ▪ *[239, n]*

■ ثُعْبَان □ <m> ■ |ṯuʿbān| □ /θuʕ.baːn/

frog ▪ *[240, n]*

■ ضِفْدِع □ <m> ■ |ḍifdiʿ| □ /dˤif.diʕ/

bird ▪ *[241, n]*

■ طَائِر □ <m> ■ |ṭāʾir| □ /tˤaːʔir/

chicken ▪ *[242, n]*

■ دَجَاجَة □ <f> ■ |dajāja| □ /da.d͡ʒaː.d͡ʒa/

duck ▪ *[243, n]*

■ بَطَّة □ <f> ■ |baṭṭa| □ /batˤ.tˤa/

fish ▪ *[244, n]*

■ سَمَكَة □ <f sgv> ■ |samaka| □ /ˈsamaka/
■ سَمَك □ <m col> ■ |samak| □ /ˈsæmæk/

insect ▪ *[245, n]*

■ حَشَرَة □ <f> ■ |ḥašara|

fly ▪ *[246, n]*

■ ذُبَابَة □ <f> ■ |ḏubāba|

body ▪ *[247, n]*

■ بَدَن □ <m> ■ |badan|

back ▪ *[248, n]* ▪ *of body*

■ ظَهْر □ <m> ■ |ẓahr| □ /ðˤa.ha.ra/ □ {of verb}

belly ▪ *[249, n]*

■ مَعِدَة □ <f> ■ |maʿida|

chest ▪ *[250, n]*

■ صَدْر □ <m> ■ |ṣadr| □ /sˤa.da.ra/ □ {of verb}

head ▪ *[251, n]*

■ رَأْس □ <m> ■ |raʾs|

neck ▪ *[252, n]*

■ رَقَبَة □ <f> ■ |raqaba|

31

foot ▪ *[253, n]* ▪ *of body*

　　　　▪ رِجْل □ <f> ▪ | rijl | □ /ra.d͡ʒi.la/ □ {of verb}

leg ▪ *[254, n]*

　　　　▪ رِجْل □ <f> ▪ | rijl | □ /ra.d͡ʒi.la/ □ {of verb}

arm ▪ *[255, n]*

　　　　▪ ذِرَاع □ <m/f> ▪ | ḏirāʿ | □ /ði.raːʕ/

finger ▪ *[256, n]*

　　　　▪ إِصْبَع □ <m> ▪ | ʼiṣbaʿ | □ /ʔiṣ.baʕ/

hand ▪ *[257, n]*

　　　　▪ يَد □ <f> ▪ | yad | □ /jad/

blood ▪ *[258, n]*

　　　　▪ دِمَاء □ <pl> ▪ | dimāʼ |

heart ▪ *[259, n]*

　　　　▪ قَلْب □ <m> ▪ | qalb | □ /qalb/

brain ▪ *[260, n]*

　　　　▪ مُخّ □ <m> ▪ | muḵḵ |

stomach ▪ *[261, n]*

　　　　▪ مَعِدَة □ <f> ▪ | maʿida |

skin ▪ *[262, n]*

　　　　▪ جِلْد □ <m> ▪ | jild |

bone ▪ *[263, n]*

　　　　▪ عَظْم □ <m> ▪ | ʿaẓm | □ /ʕað̣m/

tooth ▪ *[264, n]*

　　　　▪ سِنّ □ <f> ▪ | sinn |

health ▪ *[265, n]*

　　　　▪ صِحَّة □ <f> ▪ | ṣiḥḥa | □ /sˁiħ.ħa/

disease ▪ *[266, n]*

　　　　▪ مَرَض ▪ | maraḍ |

pain ▪ *[267, n]*

　　　　▪ أَلَم □ <m> ▪ | ʼalam |

cold ▪ *[268, n]*

　　　　▪ زُكَام □ <m> ▪ | zukām | □ /zu.kaːm/

medicine ▪ *[269, n]*

　　　　▪ دَوَاء □ <m> ▪ | dawāʼ |

spectacles ▪ *[270, n]*

　　　　▪ نَظَّارَات □ <pl> ▪ | naẓẓārāt |

hospital ▪ *[271, n]*

　　　　▪ مُسْتَشْفًى □ <m> ▪ | mustašfan | □ /mus.taʃ.fan/

doctor ▪ *[272, n]*

　　　　▪ طَبِيب □ <m> ▪ | ṭabīb |

cigarette ▪ *[273, n]*

　　　　▪ سِيجَارَة □ <f> ▪ | sījāra |

32

face ▪ *[274, n]*

▪ وَجْه □ <m> ▪ |wajh|

eye ▪ *[275, n]*

▪ عَيْن □ <f> ▪ |ˈayn|

ear ▪ *[276, n]*

▪ أُذُن □ <f> ▪ |ˈuḏun| □ /ʔu.ðun/

nose ▪ *[277, n]*

▪ أَنْف □ <m> ▪ |ˈanf|

mouth ▪ *[278, n]*

▪ فَم □ <m> ▪ |fam|

hair ▪ *[279, n]*

▪ شَعْر ▪ |šaˈr| □ /ʃa.ʕar/

food ▪ *[280, n]*

▪ أُكْل □ <m> ▪ |ˈukl| □ /ʔa.ka.la/ □ {of verb}

breakfast ▪ *[281, n]*

▪ إِفْطَار □ <m> ▪ |ˈifṭār|

lunch ▪ *[282, n]*

▪ غَدَاء □ <m> ▪ |ḡadāʾ|

dinner ▪ *[283, n]*

▪ عَشَاء □ <m> ▪ |ˈašāʾ| □ /ʕaʃaːʔ \ ʕiʃaːʔ/ □ {one may be incorrect}

cook ▪ *[284, n]*

▪ طَبَّاخ □ <m> ▪ |ṭabbāḵ| □ /tˤab.baːx/

salad ▪ *[285, n]*

▪ سَلَطَة □ <f> ▪ |salaṭa| □ /sul.tˤa \ sa.la.tˤa/ □ {one may be incorrect}

sandwich ▪ *[286, n]*

▪ سَانْدوِيتْش □ <m> ▪ |sandawitš| □ /sandwitʃ/

soup ▪ *[287, n]*

▪ شُورَبَة □ <f> ▪ |šūraba|

onion ▪ *[288, n]*

▪ بَصَل □ <m> ▪ |baṣal|

tomato ▪ *[289, n]*

▪ بَنْدُورَة □ <f> ▪ |bandūra|

potato ▪ *[290, n]*

▪ بَطَاطَا □ <f> ▪ |baṭāṭā|

apple ▪ *[291, n]*

▪ تُفَّاحَة □ <f sgv> ▪ |tuffāḥa| □ /tuf.faː.ħa/

▪ تُفَّاح □ <m col> ▪ |tuffāḥ| □ /tuf.faːħ/

orange ▪ *[292, n]*

▪ بُرْتُقَالَة □ <f sgv> ▪ |burtuqāla|

▪ بُرْتُقَال □ <m col> ▪ |burtuqāl| □ /bur.tu.qaːl/

grape • *[293, n]*
- عِنَب ▫ <m> ▪ |ʿinab|

nut • *[294, n]*
- جَوْزَة ▫ <f> ▪ |jawza|

rice • *[295, n]*
- أَرُزّ ▫ <m> ▪ |ʾaruzz|

bread • *[296, n]*
- خُبْز ▫ <m> ▪ |ḵubz| ▫ /xa.ba.za/ ▫ {of verb}

cheese • *[297, n]*
- جُبْنَة ▫ <f> ▪ |jubna|

milk • *[298, n]*
- حَلِيب ▫ <m> ▪ |ḥalīb|

egg • *[299, n]*
- بَيْضَة ▫ <f> ▪ |bayḍa|

meat • *[300, n]*
- لَحْم ▫ <m> ▪ |laḥm| ▫ /laħm/

sausage • *[301, n]*
- سُجُق ▫ <m> ▪ |sujuq|

cake • *[302, n]*
- كَعْكَة ▫ <f> ▪ |kaʿka|

chocolate • *[303, n]*
- شُوكولاتة ▫ <f> ▪ |šokolāta| ▫ /ʃu.kuː.laː.ta/

sugar • *[304, n]*
- سُكَّر ▫ <m> ▪ |sukkar|

sauce • *[305, n]*
- صَلْصَة ▫ <f> ▪ |ṣalṣa|

spice • *[306, n]*
- بَهَار ▫ <m> ▪ |bahār|

salt • *[307, n]*
- مِلْح ▫ <m> ▪ |milḥ| ▫ /milħ/

coffee • *[308, n]*
- قَهْوَة ▫ <f> ▪ |qahwa| ▫ /qah.wa/

tea • *[309, n]*
- شَاي ▫ <m> ▪ |šāy| ▫ /ʃaːj/

beer • *[310, n]*
- بِيرَة ▫ <f> ▪ |bīra|

wine • *[311, n]*
- نَبِيذ ▫ <m> ▪ |nabīḏ|

restaurant • *[312, n]*
- مَطْعَم ▫ <m> ▪ |maṭʿam| ▫ /maʃ.ʕam/

dream • *[313, n]*
- حُلْم ▫ <m> ▪ |ḥulm|

feeling ▪ *[314, n]*
- شُعُور <pl> ▪ |šuʻūr|

information ▪ *[315, n]*
- مَعْلُومَات <f pl> ▪ |maʻlūmāt|

news ▪ *[316, n]*
- أَخْبَار <pl> ▪ |ʼakbār|

memory ▪ *[317, n]*
- ذَاكِرَة <f> ▪ |dākira| ▫ /ðaː.ki.ra/

mind ▪ *[318, n]*
- عَقْل <m> ▪ |ʻaql| ▫ /ʕaq.lun/

reason ▪ *[319, n]*
- سَبَب <m> ▪ |sabab|

result ▪ *[320, n]*
- نَتِيجَة <f> ▪ |natīja|

topic ▪ *[321, n]*
- مَوْضُوع <m> ▪ |mawḍūʻ| ▫ /maw.dˤuːʕ/

thought ▪ *[322, n]*
- فِكْر <m> ▪ |fikr|

list ▪ *[323, n]*
- قَائِمَة <f> ▪ |qāʼima| ▫ /qaː.ʔi.ma/

number ▪ *[324, n]* ▪ *of rank*
- رَقْم <m> ▪ |raqm| ▫ /raqm/

kind ▪ *[325, n]*
- نَوْع ▪ |nawʻ|

text ▪ *[326, n]*
- نَصّ <m> ▪ |naṣṣ| ▫ /nasˤsˤ/

letter ▪ *[327, n]* ▪ *message*
- رِسَالَة <f> ▪ |risāla| ▫ /ri.saː.la/

book ▪ *[328, n]*
- كِتَاب <m> ▪ |kitāb| ▫ [keˈtæːb]

map ▪ *[329, n]*
- خَرِيطَة <f> ▪ |karīṭa| ▫ /xa.riː.tˤa/

dictionary ▪ *[330, n]*
- قَامُوس <m> ▪ |qāmūs| ▫ /qaː.muːs/

page ▪ *[331, n]*
- صَفْحَة <f> ▪ |ṣafḥa|

library ▪ *[332, n]*
- مَكْتَبَة <f> ▪ |maktaba| ▫ /mak.ta.ba/

pen ▪ *[333, n]*
- قَلَم <m> ▪ |qalam| ▫ /qa.la.ma/ ▫ {of verb}

letter ▪ *[334, n]* ▪ *symbol*
- حَرْف <m> ▪ |ḥarf| ▫ /ħarf/

number ▪ [335, n] ▪ symbol
> ▪ عَدَد □ \<m\> ▪ |ˈadad| □ /ˈa.dad/

flag ▪ [336, n]
> ▪ عَلَم □ \<m\> ▪ |ˈalam| □ /ˈa.li.aˈ/ □ {of verb}

name ▪ [337, n]
> ▪ اِسْم □ \<m\> ▪ |ism| □ /ism/

word ▪ [338, n]
> ▪ كَلِمَة □ \<f\> ▪ |kalima| □ /ka.li.ma/

sentence ▪ [339, n]
> ▪ جُمْلَة □ \<f\> ▪ |jumla| □ /d͡ʒum.la/

language ▪ [340, n]
> ▪ لُغَة □ \<f\> ▪ |luḡa| □ /lu.ɣa/

goal ▪ [341, n]
> ▪ هَدَف □ \<m\> ▪ |hadaf|

problem ▪ [342, n]
> ▪ مُشْكِلَة □ \<f\> ▪ |muškila|

mistake ▪ [343, n]
> ▪ خَطَأ □ \<f\> ▪ |ḵaṭa'|

habit ▪ [344, n]
> ▪ عَادَة □ \<f\> ▪ |ˈāda| □ /ˈa:.da/

voice ▪ [345, n]
> ▪ صَوْت □ \<m\> ▪ |ṣawt|

message ▪ [346, n]
> ▪ رِسَالَة □ \<f\> ▪ |risāla| □ /ri.sa:.la/

story ▪ [347, n]
> ▪ قِصَّة □ \<f\> ▪ |qiṣṣa|

human ▪ [348, n]
> ▪ إِنْسَان □ \<m\> ▪ |ˈinsān| □ /ˈin.sa:n/

culture ▪ [349, n]
> ▪ ثَقَافَة □ \<f\> ▪ |ṯaqāfa| □ /θa.qa:.fa/

nation ▪ [350, n]
> ▪ أُمَّة □ \<f\> ▪ |ˈumma|

people ▪ [351, n]
> ▪ نَاس □ \<pl\> ▪ |nās|

team ▪ [352, n]
> ▪ فَرِيق □ \<m\> ▪ |farīq| □ /fa.ri:q/

baby ▪ [353, n]
> ▪ رَضِيع □ \<m\> ▪ |raḍī'|

boy ▪ [354, n]
> ▪ صَبِيّ □ \<m\> ▪ |ṣabiyy|

man ▪ [355, n]
> ▪ راجل □ \<m\> ▪ |ṛažel| □ /ra:.d͡ʒil/

girl ▪ *[356, n]*

▪ بِنْت ▫ <f> ▪ |bint| ▫ /bint/

woman ▪ *[357, n]*

▪ اِمْرَأَة ▫ <f> ▪ |imra'a| ▫ /ʔim.ra.ʔa/

husband ▪ *[358, n]*

▪ زَوْج ▫ <m> ▪ |zawj| ▫ /zawd͡ʒ/

wife ▪ *[359, n]*

▪ زَوْجَة ▫ <f> ▪ |zawja| ▫ /zawd͡ʒa/

family ▪ *[360, n]*

▪ عَائِلَة ▫ <f> ▪ |'ā'ila| ▫ /ʕaː.ʔi.la/

father ▪ *[361, n]*

▪ أَب ▫ <m> ▪ |'ab| ▫ /ʔab/

mother ▪ *[362, n]*

▪ أُمّ ▫ <f> ▪ |'umm| ▫ /ʔam.ma/ ▫ {of verb}

daughter ▪ *[363, n]*

▪ اِبْنَة ▫ <f> ▪ |ibna|

son ▪ *[364, n]*

▪ اِبْن ▫ <m> ▪ |ibn| ▫ /ibn \ ib.ni/ ▫ {one may be incorrect}

sister ▪ *[366, n]*

▪ أُخْت ▫ <f> ▪ |'uḵt| ▫ /ʔuxt/

aunt ▪ *[367, n]*

▪ عَمَّة ▫ <f> ▫ {paternal} ▪ |'amma| ▫ /ʕim.ma \ ʕam.ma/ ▫ {one may be incorrect}

▪ خَالَة ▫ <f> ▫ {maternal} ▪ |ḵāla|

uncle ▪ *[368, n]*

▪ عَمّ ▫ <m> ▫ {paternal} ▪ |'amm|

▪ خَال ▫ <m> ▫ {maternal} ▪ |ḵāl| ▫ /'xɛːl/ ▫ {Egyptian Arabic}

friend ▪ *[369, n]*

▪ صَدِيق ▫ <m> ▪ |ṣadīq| ▫ /sˤa.diːq/

neighbour ▪ *[370, n]*

▪ جَار ▫ <m> ▪ |jār|

guest ▪ *[371, n]*

▪ ضَيْف ▫ <m/f> ▪ |ḍayf|

enemy ▪ *[372, n]*

▪ عَدُو ▫ <m> ▪ |'adū| ▫ /ʕa.duww/

religion ▪ *[373, n]*

▪ دِيَانة ▫ <f> ▪ |diyāna|

priest ▪ *[374, n]*

▪ قِسِّيس ▫ <m> ▪ |qissīs| ▫ /qis.siːs/

temple ▪ *[375, n]*

god • *[376, n]*

■ مَعْبَد ▫ <m> ▪ |maʻbad|

art • *[377, n]*

■ إِله ▫ <m> ▪ |ʾilāh| ▫ [ʔeˈlæːh]

picture • *[378, n]*

■ فَنّ ▫ <m> ▪ |fann|

photograph • *[379, n]*

■ صُورَة ▫ <f> ▪ |ṣūra| ▫ /sˤuː.ra/

museum • *[380, n]*

■ صُورَة ▫ <f> ▪ |ṣūra| ▫ /sˤuː.ra/

music • *[381, n]*

■ مُتْحَف ▫ <m> ▪ |matḥaf|

song • *[382, n]*

■ مُوسِيقَى ▫ <f> ▪ |mūsīqā| ▫ /muː.siː.qaː/

guitar • *[383, n]*

■ أُغْنِيَّة ▫ <f> ▪ |ʾuġniyya|

piano • *[384, n]*

■ قِيثَارَة ▫ <f> ▪ |qīṯāra| ▫ /qiː.θaː.ra/

drum • *[385, n]*

■ بِيَانُو ▫ <m> ▪ |biyānō|

musician • *[386, n]*

■ طَبَل ▫ <m> ▪ |ṭabala|

literature • *[387, n]*

■ مُوسِيقِيّ ▫ <m> ▪ |mūsīqiyy|

movie • *[388, n]*

■ أَدَب ▫ <m> ▪ |ʾadab| ▫ /ʔa.dab/

actor • *[389, n]*

■ فِيلْم ▫ <m> ▪ |film| ▫ /fɪlm/

theater • *[390, n]*

■ مُمَثِّل ▫ <m> ▪ |mumaṯṯil|

television • *[391, n]* • *medium*

■ مَسْرَح ▫ <m> ▪ |masraḥ| ▫ /mas.raħ/

newspaper • *[392, n]*

■ تِلْفَاز ▫ <m> ▪ |tilfāz|

education • *[393, n]*

■ جَرِيدَة ▫ <f> ▪ |jarīda| ▫ /d͡ʒa.riː.da/

school • *[394, n]*

■ تَعْلِيم ▫ <m> ▪ |taʻlīm|

university • *[395, n]*

■ مَدْرَسَة ▫ <f> ▪ |madrasa| ▫ /mad.ra.sa \ mu.dar.ri.sa/ ▫ {one may be incorrect}

■ جَامِعَة ▫ <f> ▪ |jāmiʻa| ▫ /d͡ʒaː.mi.ʕa/

science ▪ *[396, n]*

▪ عِلْم ▫ <m> ▪ |ˈilm| ▫ /ˈa.li.aʕ/ {of verb}

teacher ▪ *[397, n]*

▪ مُعَلِّم ▫ <m> ▪ |muˈallim| ▫ /mil.ʕam / mu.ʕal.lim \ maʕ.lam \ muʕ.lim/ ▫ {one may be incorrect}

student ▪ *[398, n]*

▪ طَالِب ▫ <m> ▪ |ṭālib| ▫ /tˤaː.lib/

address ▪ *[399, n]*

▪ عُنْوَان ▫ <m> ▪ |ˈunwān| ▫ /ʕun.waːn/

post office ▪ *[400, n]*

▪ أَلْبَرِيد مَكْتَب ▫ <m> ▪ |maktab al-barīd|

money ▪ *[401, n]*

▪ نُقُود ▫ <pl> ▪ |nuqūd|

coin ▪ *[402, n]*

▪ قِرْش ▫ <m> ▪ |qirš|

bank ▪ *[403, n]*

▪ مَصرِف ▫ <m> ▪ |maṣrif|

salary ▪ *[404, n]*

▪ رَاتِب ▫ <m> ▪ |rātib|

tax ▪ *[405, n]*

▪ رِيبَةضَ ▫ <f> ▪ |ḍarība| ▫ /dˤa.riː.ba/

company ▪ *[406, n]*

▪ شَرِكَة ▫ <f> ▪ |šarika| ▫ /ʃa.ri.ka/

job ▪ *[407, n]*

▪ عَمَل ▫ <m> ▪ |ˈamal|

manager ▪ *[408, n]*

▪ مُدِير ▫ <m> ▪ |mudīr| ▫ /mu.diːr/

worker ▪ *[409, n]*

▪ عَامِل ▫ <m> ▪ |ˈāmil| ▫ /ʕaː.ma.la/ {of verb}

shop ▪ *[410, n]*

▪ دُكَّان ▫ <m> ▪ |dukkān| ▫ /duk.kaːn/

price ▪ *[411, n]*

▪ ثَمَن ▫ <m> ▪ |ṯaman|

gift ▪ *[412, n]*

▪ هَدِيَّة ▫ <f> ▪ |hadiyya| ▫ /ha.dij.ja/

factory ▪ *[413, n]*

▪ مَصْنَع ▫ <m> ▪ |maṣnaˈ| ▫ /mas.ˤnaʕ/ /ʕan.ˤam/

engineer ▪ *[414, n]*

▪ مُهَنْدِس ▫ <m> ▪ |muhandis| ▫ /mu.han.dis/

farm ▪ *[415, n]*

▪ مَزْرَعَة ▫ <f> ▪ |mazraˈa| ▫ /maz.ra.ʕa/

farmer ▪ *[416, n]*

- فَلَّاح ▫ <m> ▪ |fallāḥ| ▫ /fal.laːħ/

tool ▪ *[417, n]*

- أَدَاة ▫ <f> ▪ |ʾadāh|

scissors ▪ *[418, n]*

- مِقَصّ ▫ <m> ▪ |miqaṣṣ| ▫ /mi.qasˤsˤ/

brush ▪ *[419, n]*

- فُرْشَاة ▫ <f> ▪ |furšāh| ▫ /fur.ʃaːh/

key ▪ *[420, n]*

- مِفْتَاح ▫ <m> ▪ |miftāḥ|

lock ▪ *[421, n]*

- قِفْل ▫ <m> ▪ |qifl|

document ▪ *[422, n]*

- وَثِيقَة ▫ <f> ▪ |watīqa| ▫ /wa.θiː.qa/

passport ▪ *[423, n]*

- سَفَر وَازجَ ▫ <m> ▪ |jawāz safar| ▫ /d͡ʒa.waːz sa.far/

receipt ▪ *[424, n]*

- إِيصَال ▫ <m> ▪ |ʾīṣāl|

law ▪ *[425, n]*

- قَانُون ▫ <m> ▪ |qānūn| ▫ /qaː.nuːn/

right ▪ *[426, n]*

- حَق ▫ <m> ▪ |ḥaq| ▫ /ħaq.qa/ ▫ {of verb}

criminal ▪ *[427, n]*

- مُجْرِم ▫ <m> ▪ |mujrim|

police ▪ *[428, n]*

- شُرْطَة ▫ <f> ▪ |šurṭa| ▫ /ʃur.tˤa \ ʃar.tˤa/ ▫ {one may be incorrect}

police officer ▪ *[429, n]*

- شُرْطِيّ ▫ <m> ▪ |šurṭiyy|

lawyer ▪ *[430, n]*

- مُحَامٍ ▫ <m> ▪ |muḥāmin| ▫ /mu.ħaː.min/

prison ▪ *[431, n]*

- سِجْن ▫ <m> ▪ |sijn|

politician ▪ *[432, n]*

- سِيَاسِيّ ▫ <m> ▪ |siyāsiyy|

president ▪ *[433, n]*

- رَئِيس ▫ <m> ▪ |raʾīs|

king ▪ *[434, n]*

- مَلِك ▫ <m> ▪ |malik| ▫ /ma.lik \ mulk \ milk/ ▫ {one may be incorrect}

army ▪ *[435, n]*

- جَيْش ▫ <m> ▪ |jayš| ▫ /d͡ʒajʃ/

soldier ▪ *[436, n]*

▪ جُنْدِيّ ▫ <m> ▪ |jundiyy|

castle ▪ *[437, n]*

▪ قَلْعَة ▫ <f> ▪ |qalʻa| ▫ /qal.ʕa/

war ▪ *[438, n]*

▪ حَرْب ▫ <f> ▪ |ḥarb|

peace ▪ *[439, n]*

▪ سَلَام ▫ <m> ▪ |salām|

sword ▪ *[440, n]*

▪ سَيْف ▫ <m> ▪ |sayf| ▫ /siːf/

gun ▪ *[441, n]*

▪ مُسَدَّس ▫ <m> ▪ |musaddas| ▫ /mu.sad.das/

bomb ▪ *[442, n]*

▪ قُنْبُلَة ▫ <f> ▪ |qunbula|

sport ▪ *[443, n]*

▪ رِيَاضَة ▫ <f> ▪ |riyāḍa|

stadium ▪ *[444, n]*

▪ مَلْعَب ▫ <m> ▪ |malʻab|

dance ▪ *[445, n]*

▪ رَقْص ▫ <m> ▪ |raqṣ|

game ▪ *[446, n]*

▪ لَعْب ▫ <m> ▪ |laʻb|

chess ▪ *[447, n]*

▪ شَطْرَنْج ▫ <m> ▪ |šaṭranj|

toy ▪ *[448, n]*

▪ لُعْبَة ▫ <f> ▪ |luʻba|

ball ▪ *[449, n]*

▪ كُرَة ▫ <f> ▪ |kura|

not ▪ *[450, sv]*

▪ لَا ▪ |lā|

can ▪ *[451, sv]*

▪ قَدَر ▪ |qadara|

must ▪ *[453, sv]*

▪ وَجَب ▪ |wajaba| ▫ /wa.d͡ʒa.ba/

be ▪ *[454, v]* ▪ **subject equals objeCT**

▪ كَانَ ▫ {present tense seldom used} ▪ |kāna| ▫ /kaː.na/

be ▪ *[455, v]* ▪ *to exist*

▪ كَانَ ▫ {present tense seldom used} ▪ |kāna| ▫ /kaː.na/

live ▪ *[456, v]*

▪ عَاشَ ▪ |ʻāša| ▫ /ʕaː.ʃa/

die ▪ *[457, v]*

▪ مَاتَ ▫ <pf> ▪ |māta| ▫ /ˈmaːta/

disappear ▪ *[459, v]*

41

• اِخْتَفَى • | iḵtafā |

do • [460, v]

• فَعَلَ • | faʻala | ▫ /fa.ʕa.la/

rest • [461, v]

• اِسْتَرَاحَ • | istarāḥa |

create • [462, v]

• خَلَقَ • | ḵalaqa | ▫ /xa.la.qa/

change • [463, v] • to make into different

• غَيَّرَ • | ḡayyara | ▫ /ɣaj.ja.ra/

become • [464, v]

• أَصْبَحَ • | ʼaṣbaḥa |

join • [465, v]

• اِنْضَمَّ • | inḍamma |

break • [466, v] • to separate

• كَسَرَ • | kasara |

remove • [468, v]

• نَقَلَ • | naqala |

leave • [469, v] • to cause to remain

• تَرَكَ • | taraka | ▫ /ta.ra.ka/

grow • [470, v]

• نَمَى • | namā |

open • [471, v]

• فَتَحَ • | fataḥa | ▫ /fa.ta.ħa/

close • [472, v]

• أَغْلَقَ • | ʼaḡlaqa |

measure • [473, v]

• قَاسَ • | qāsa |

boil • [474, v]

• غَلَى • | ḡalā |

light • [476, v]

• شَعَّلَ • | šaʻʻala |

burn • [477, v]

• حَرَقَ • | ḥaraqa |

be • [478, v] • to occupy place

▫ كَانَ {present tense seldom used} • | kāna | ▫ /kaː.na/

cover • [479, v]

• غَطَّى • | ḡaṭṭā |

move • [480, v]

• حَرَكَ • | ḥaraka |

stop • [481, v] • to cease moving

• تَوَقَّفَ • | tawaqqafa | ▫ /ta.waq.qa.fa/

stay • [482, v]

▪ مَكَثَ ▪ | makaṯa |

go ▪ [483, v]

▪ ذَهَبَ ▪ | ḏahaba | ▫ /ða.ha.ba/

return ▪ [485, v]

▪ رَجَعَ ▪ | rajaʻa | ▫ /ra.d͡ʒa.ʕa/

leave ▪ [486, v] ▪ to depart

▪ تَرَكَ ▪ | taraka | ▫ /ta.ra.ka/

arrive ▪ [487, v]

▪ وَصَلَ ▪ | waṣala |

enter ▪ [488, v]

▪ دَخَلَ ▪ | daḵala | ▫ /da.xa.la/

come ▪ [489, v]

▪ جَاءَ ▪ | jāʼa | ▫ /d͡ʒaː.ʔa/

follow ▪ [490, v]

▪ تَبِعَ ▪ | tabiʻa |

walk ▪ [491, v]

▪ مَشَى ▪ | mašā | ▫ /ma.ʃaː/

run ▪ [492, v]

▪ رَكَضَ ▪ | rakaḍa | ▫ /ra.ka.dˤa/

swim ▪ [493, v]

▪ سَبَحَ ▪ | sabaḥa |

fly ▪ [494, v]

▪ طَارَ ▪ | ṭāra |

travel ▪ [495, v]

▪ سَافَرَ ▪ | sāfara |

fall ▪ [496, v]

▪ وَقَعَ ▪ | waqaʻa | ▫ /wa.qa.ʕa/

jump ▪ [497, v]

▪ قَفَزَ ▪ | qafaza |

pull ▪ [498, v]

▪ جَرَّ ▪ | jarra |

push ▪ [499, v]

▪ دَفَعَ ▪ | dafaʻa |

throw ▪ [500, v]

▪ صَبَّ ▪ | ṣabba |

stand ▪ [501, v]

▪ وَقَفَ ▪ | waqafa |

sit ▪ [502, v]

▪ جَلَسَ ▪ | jalasa | ▫ /d͡ʒa.la.sa/

lie ▪ [503, v]

▪ رَقَدَ ▪ | raqada |

hang ▪ [504, v]

■ قَعَلَّ ■ |ʻallaqa|

touch ▪ [505, v]

■ لَمَسَ ■ |lamasa| ▫ /lɛms/ ▫ {Egyptian Arabic; of noun}

hit ▪ [506, v]

■ ضَرَبَ ■ |ḍaraba|

support ▪ [507, v]

■ دَعَمَ ■ |daʻama|

receive ▪ [508, v]

■ اِسْتَقْبَلَ ■ |istaqbala|

take ▪ [509, v]

■ أَخَذَ ■ |ʼak̲aḏa| ▫ /ʔa.xa.ða/

collect ▪ [510, v]

■ جَمَعَ ■ |jamaʻa| ▫ /d͡ʒa.ma.ʕa/

lend ▪ [511, v]

■ أَعَارَ ■ |ʼaʻāra|

give ▪ [512, v]

■ يُعْطِي أَعْطَى ■ |ʼaʻṭā|

share ▪ [513, v]

■ شَارَكَ ■ |šāraka|

carry ▪ [514, v]

■ حَمَلَ ■ |ḥamala|

bring ▪ [515, v]

■ أَحْضَرَ ■ |ʼaḥḍara|

send ▪ [516, v]

■ أَرْسَلَ ■ |ʼarsala|

have ▪ [517, v]

■ مَلَكَ ■ |malaka| ▫ /ma.la.ka/
■ {usually no verb is used, prepositions - عِنْدَ |ʻinda|, لِـ |li-|, etc. + noun or pronoun are used, e. g. عِنْدِي |ʻindī| - I have, عِنْدَكَ |ʻindak| - you have, etc.} ■

own ▪ [518, v]

■ مَلَكَ ■ |malaka| ▫ /ma.la.ka/

lose ▪ [519, v] ▪ to cease possesion

■ فَقَدَ ■ |faqada|

keep ▪ [520, v]

■ اِحْتَفَظَ ■ |iḥtafaẓa|

hold ▪ [521, v]

■ مَسَكَ ■ |masaka|

need ▪ [523, v]

■ حْتَاجَا ■ |iḥtāja|

prepare ▪ [524, v]

■ جَهَّزَ ■ |jahhaza|

use ▪ *[525, v]*

▪ اِسْتَعْمَلَ ▪ |istaʿmala|

destroy ▪ *[526, v]*

▪ دَمَّرَ ▪ |dammara|

repair ▪ *[528, v]*

▪ أَصْلَحَ ▪ |ʾaṣlaḥa|

clean ▪ *[529, v]*

▪ نَظَّفَ ▪ |naẓẓafa|

wash ▪ *[530, v]*

▪ سَلَغَ ▪ |ḡasala|

shave ▪ *[531, v]*

▪ شَعْر حَلَقَ ▪ |ḥalaqa šaʿr|

defend ▪ *[532, v]*

▪ حَمَى ▪ |ḥamā|

save ▪ *[533, v]* ▪ **to help to survive**

▪ أَنْقَذَ ▪ |ʾanqaḏa|

prevent ▪ *[534, v]*

▪ مَنَعَ ▪ |manaʿa|

begin ▪ *[535, v]*

▪ بَدَأَ ▪ |badaʾa| ▫ /ba.da.ʔa/

continue ▪ *[536, v]*

▪ تَابَعَ ▫ <tr> ▪ |tābaʿa|

▪ دَامَ ▫ <intr> ▪ |dāma|

finish ▪ *[537, v]*

▪ فَرَغَ ▪ |faraḡa| ▫ /fa.ra.ɣa/

stop ▪ *[538, v]* ▪ **to cause to end**

▪ أَوْقَفَ ▪ |ʾawqafa| ▫ /ʔaw.qa.fa/

wait ▪ *[539, v]*

▪ اِنْتَظَرَ ▪ |intaẓara|

delay ▪ *[540, v]*

▪ سَوَّفَ ▪ |sawwafa|

drive ▪ *[541, v]*

▪ قَادَ ▪ |qāda|

wear ▪ *[543, v]*

▪ لَبِسَ ▪ |labisa|

breathe ▪ *[544, v]*

▪ تَنَفَّسَ ▪ |tanaffasa|

cough ▪ *[545, v]*

▪ سَعَلَ ▪ |saʿala|

kiss ▪ *[546, v]*

▪ قَبَّلَ ▪ |qabbala|

fuck ▪ *[547, v]*

hurt ▪ *[548, v]*

- نَاكَ ▪ |nāka|

cure ▪ *[549, v]*

- أَلِمَ ▪ |ʾalima|

smoke ▪ *[550, v]*

- شَفَى ▪ |šafā|

drink ▪ *[552, v]*

- دَخَّنَ ▪ |dakkana|

feed ▪ *[553, v]*

- شَرِبَ ▪ |šariba| ▫ /ʃa.ri.ba/

cook ▪ *[554, v]*

- غَذَّى ▪ |ḡaḏḏā| ▫ /ɣað.ða:/

sleep ▪ *[555, v]*

- طَبَخَ ▪ |ṭabaka|

dream ▪ *[557, v]*

- نَامَ ▪ |nāma| ▫ /na:.ma/

look ▪ *[558, v]*

- حَلَمَ ▪ |ḥalama|

see ▪ *[559, v]*

- نَظَرَ ▪ |naẓara| ▫ /na.ðˤa.ra/

listen ▪ *[560, v]*

- رَأَى ▪ |raʾā| ▫ /ra.ʔa:/

hear ▪ *[561, v]*

- أَصْغَى ▪ |ʾaṣḡā| ▫ /ʔasˤ.ɣa:/

taste ▪ *[562, v]*

- سَمِعَ ▪ |samiʿa|

smell ▪ *[563, v]*

- تَذَوَّقَ ▪ |taḏawwaqa|

search ▪ *[564, v]*

- شَمَّ ▪ |šamma| ▫ /ʃam.ma/

find ▪ *[565, v]*

- بَحَثَ ▪ |baḥaṯa| ▫ /ba.ħa.θa/

discover ▪ *[566, v]*

- وَجَدَ ▪ |wajada|

hide ▪ *[567, v]*

- اِكْتَشَفَ ▪ |iktašafa|

mean ▪ *[568, v]*

- أَخْفَى ▪ |ʾakfā|

remember ▪ *[569, v]* ▪ *to memorize*

- عَنَى ▪ |ʿanā|

remember ▪ *[570, v]* ▪ *to recall*

- اِسْتَذْكَرَ ▪ |istaḏkara|

‧ تَذَكَّرَ ‧ |taḏakkara|

know ‧ *[571, v]* ‧ *to be acquainted with*

‧ عَرَفَ ‧ |ˈarafa| ▫ /ʕa.ra.fa/

forget ‧ *[572, v]*

‧ نَسِيَ ‧ |nasiya|

understand ‧ *[573, v]*

‧ فَهِمَ ‧ |fahima|

think ‧ *[574, v]*

‧ فَكَرَ ‧ |fakara|

know ‧ *[575, v]* ‧ *to be sure about*

‧ عَلِمَ ‧ |ˈalima| ▫ /ʕa.li.ma/

believe ‧ *[576, v]*

‧ صَدَّقَ ‧ |ṣaddaqa| ▫ /ˈsˤadaqa/

seem ‧ *[577, v]*

‧ بَدَا ‧ |badā|

guess ‧ *[578, v]*

‧ خَمَّنَ ‧ |ḵammana|

arrange ‧ *[579, v]*

‧ رَتَّبَ ‧ |rattaba|

count ‧ *[580, v]*

‧ يَعُدُّ عَدَّ ‧ |ˈadda|

invent ‧ *[581, v]*

‧ اِخْتَرَعَ ‧ |iḵtaraˈa|

name ‧ *[582, v]*

‧ سَمَّى ‧ |sammā|

compare ‧ *[583, v]*

‧ قَارَنَ ‧ |qārana|

read ‧ *[584, v]*

‧ قَرَأَ ‧ |qaraˈa| ▫ /qa.ra.ʔa/

write ‧ *[585, v]*

‧ كَتَبَ ‧ |kataba| ▫ /ka.ta.ba/

print ‧ *[586, v]*

‧ طَبَعَ ‧ |ṭabaˈa|

spell ‧ *[587, v]*

‧ تَهَجَّأَ ‧ |tahajjaˈa|

translate ‧ *[588, v]*

‧ تَرْجَمَ ‧ |tarjama| ▫ /ˈtardʒama/

mark ‧ *[589, v]*

‧ أَشَّرَ ‧ |ˈaššara|

feel ‧ *[590, v]*

‧ شَعَرَ ‧ |šaˈara| ▫ /ʃa.ʕa.ra/

laugh ‧ *[591, v]*

47

smile ▪ *[592, v]*	▪ ضَحِكَ ▪ |ḍaḥika|
cry ▪ *[593, v]*	▪ إِبْتَسَمَ ▪ |ibtasama|
fear ▪ *[594, v]*	▪ بَكَى ▪ |bakā| ▫ /bu.kan/
like ▪ *[595, v]*	▪ خَافَ ▪ |ḵāfa|
miss ▪ *[596, v]*	▪ حَبَّ ▪ |ḥabba| ▫ /ħab.ba/
love ▪ *[597, v]*	▪ اِفْتَقَد ▪ |iftaqada|
want ▪ *[598, v]*	▪ حَبَّ ▪ |ḥabba| ▫ /ħab.ba/
hope ▪ *[599, v]*	▪ أَرَادَ ▪ |'arāda| ▫ /ʔa.raː.da/
hate ▪ *[600, v]*	▪ مَلَأ ▪ |'amala|
intend ▪ *[601, v]*	▪ كَرِهَ ▪ |kariha|
choose ▪ *[602, v]*	▪ تَعَمَّدَ ▪ |ta'ammada|
try ▪ *[603, v]*	▪ إِخْتَارَ ▪ |iḵtāra|
repeat ▪ *[604, v]*	▪ حَاوَلَ ▪ |ḥāwala|
speak ▪ *[607, v]*	▪ كَرَّرَ ▪ |karrara|
say ▪ *[608, v]*	▪ تَحَدَّثَ ▪ |taḥaddaṯa|
shout ▪ *[609, v]*	▪ قَالَ ▪ |qāla| ▫ /qaː.la/
whisper ▪ *[610, v]*	▪ صَرَخَ ▪ |ṣaraḵa|
tell ▪ *[611, v]*	▪ هَمَسَ ▪ |hamasa|
describe ▪ *[612, v]*	▪ أَخْبَرَ ▪ |'aḵbara|
explain ▪ *[613, v]*	▪ وَصَفَ ▪ |waṣafa|
show ▪ *[614, v]*	▪ شَرَحَ ▪ |šaraḥa|

48

talk ▪ [615, v]

▪ عَرَضَ ▪ |ʿaraḍa|

▪ تَكَلَّمَ ▪ |takallama| □ /ta.kal.la.ma/

meet ▪ [616, v]

▪ لَاقَى ▪ |lāqā|

visit ▪ [617, v]

▪ زَارَ ▪ |zāra| □ /zaː.ra/

ask ▪ [618, v]

▪ سَأَلَ ▪ |saʾala|

answer ▪ [619, v]

▪ أَجَابَ ▪ |ʾajāba| □ /ʔa.d͡ʒaː.ba/

advise ▪ [620, v]

▪ نَصَحَ ▪ |naṣaḥa|

offer ▪ [621, v]

▪ اِقْتَرَحَ ▪ |iqtaraḥa|

promise ▪ [622, v]

▪ وَعَدَ ▪ |waʿada| □ /wa.ʕa.da/

call ▪ [623, v]

▪ دَعَا ▪ |daʿā|

invite ▪ [624, v]

▪ دَعَا ▪ |daʿā|

help ▪ [625, v]

▪ سَاعَدَ ▪ |sāʿada| □ /saː.ʕa.da/

control ▪ [626, v]

▪ سَيْطَرَ ▪ |sayṭara| □ /saj.tˤa.ra/

order ▪ [627, v]

▪ أَمَرَ ▪ |ʾamara|

punish ▪ [628, v]

▪ عَاقَبَ ▪ |ʿāqaba|

agree ▪ [629, v]

▪ وَافَقَ ▪ |wāfaqa|

fight ▪ [630, v]

▪ قَاتَلَ ▪ |qātala|

attack ▪ [631, v]

▪ هَاجَمَ ▪ |hājama| □ /haː.d͡ʒa.ma/

escape ▪ [632, v]

▪ هَرَبَ ▪ |haraba|

win ▪ [633, v]

▪ فَازَ ▪ |fāza|

lose ▪ [634, v] ▪ to fail

▪ خَسِرَ ▪ |ḵasira|

pray ▪ [635, v]

- صَلَّى | ṣallā | ▫ /'sˤɑlːɑː/

draw ▪ [636, v]

- رَسَمَ | rasama |

sing ▪ [637, v]

- غَنَّى | ḡannā |

teach ▪ [638, v]

- عَلَّمَ | ʻallama | ▫ /ʕa.li.ma/

learn ▪ [639, v]

- تَعَلَّمَ | taʻallama |

sell ▪ [640, v]

- بَاعَ | bāʻa | ▫ /baː.ʕa/

buy ▪ [641, v]

- اِشْتَرَى | ištarā | ▫ /iʃ.ta.raː/

pay ▪ [642, v]

- دَفَعَ | dafaʻa |

build ▪ [643, v]

- بَنَى | banā |

shoot ▪ [644, v]

- صَوَّبَ | ṣawwaba |

hunt ▪ [645, v]

- اِصْطَادَ | iṣṭāda | ▫ /isˤ.tˤaː.da/

kill ▪ [646, v]

- قَتَلَ | qatala |

steal ▪ [647, v]

- سَرَقَ | saraqa |

dance ▪ [648, v]

- رَقَصَ | raqaṣa |

play ▪ [649, v]

- لَعِبَ | laʻiba |

alive ▪ [650, adj]

- حَيّ | ḥayy |

dead ▪ [651, adj]

- مَيِّت | mayyit |

whole ▪ [652, adj]

- كَامِل | kāmil | ▫ /kaː.mil/

common ▪ [653, adj] ▪ usual

- شَائِع | šāʼiʻ |

strange ▪ [654, adj]

- غَرِيب | ḡarīb |

general ▪ [655, adj]

- عَامّ | ʻāmm | ▫ /ʕaːmm/

special ▪ [656, adj]

• خَاصّ • |ḵāṣṣ|

simple • *[659, adj]*

• بَسِيط • |basīṭ|

empty • *[660, adj]*

• فَارِغ • |fāriḡ| ▫ /fa:.riɣ/

full • *[661, adj]* • *containing maximum*

• مُمْتَلِئ • |mumtali'|

small • *[662, adj]*

• صَغِير • |ṣaḡīr| ▫ /sˤa.ɣi:r/

big • *[663, adj]*

• كَبِير • |kabīr| ▫ /ka.bi:r/

large • *[664, adj]*

• كَبِير • |kabīr| ▫ /ka.bi:r/

short • *[665, adj]* • *of size*

• قَصِير • |qaṣīr| ▫ /qa.sˤi:r/

long • *[666, adj]* • *of size*

• طَوِيل • |ṭawīl| ▫ /tˤa.wi:l/

low • *[667, adj]*

• مُنْخَفِض • |munḵafiḍ|

high • *[668, adj]*

• عَالٍ • |ʿālin| ▫ /ʕa:.lin/

narrow • *[669, adj]*

• ضَيِّق • |ḍayyiq|

wide • *[670, adj]*

• وَاسِع • |wāsiʿ|

thin • *[671, adj]*

• رَفِيع • |rafīʿ|

thick • *[672, adj]*

• سَمِيك • |samīk|

light • *[673, adj]* • *of weight*

• خَفِيف • |ḵafīf|

heavy • *[674, adj]*

• ثَقِيل • |ṯaqīl|

dark • *[675, adj]*

• مُظْلِم • |muẓlim|

bright • *[676, adj]*

• لَامِع • |lāmiʿ|

black • *[678, adj]*

• أَسْوَد • |'aswad| ▫ /ʔas.wad/

grey • *[679, adj]*

• رَمَادِيّ • |ramādiyy| ▫ /ra.ma:.dijj/

white • *[680, adj]*

blue - *[681, adj]*

• أَبْيَض • <m> • |'abyaḍ| • /ʔab.jadˤ/

green - *[682, adj]*

• أَزْرَق • |'azraq| • /ʔaz.raq/

red - *[683, adj]*

• أَخْضَر • |'akḍar| • /ʔax.dˤar/

yellow - *[684, adj]*

• أَحْمَر • |'aḥmar| • /ʔaħ.mar/

loud - *[685, adj]*

• أَصْفَر • |'aṣfar| • /ʔasˤ.far/

quiet - *[686, adj]*

• عَلٍ • |'ālin|

hot - *[687, adj]* - *temperature*

• صَامِت • |ṣāmit|

warm - *[688, adj]*

• حَارّ • |ḥārr|

cold - *[689, adj]*

• دَافِئ • |dāfi'|

dry - *[690, adj]*

• بَارِد • |bārid|

wet - *[691, adj]*

• جَاف • |jāf|

hard - *[692, adj]*

• مَبْلُول • |mablūl|

soft - *[693, adj]*

• صُلْب • |ṣulb|

smooth - *[694, adj]*

• نَاعِم • |nā'im|

sharp - *[695, adj]*

• نَاعِم • |nā'im|

flat - *[696, adj]*

• حَادّ • |ḥād|

bitter - *[697, adj]*

• مُسَطَّح • |musaṭṭaḥ|

sour - *[699, adj]*

• مُرّ • |murr|

local - *[701, adj]*

• حَامِض • |ḥāmiḍ| • /ħɑ:miḍ/ • {Egyptian Arabic}

near - *[702, adj]*

• مَحَلِّيّ • |maḥalliyy|

far - *[703, adj]*

• قَرِيب • |qarīb| • /qa.ri:b/

▪ بَعِيد ▪ | baʿīd | ▫ /baʕiːd/

opposite ▪ *[704, adj]*

▪ ضِدّ ▪ | ḍidd |

weak ▪ *[705, adj]*

▪ ضَعِيف ▪ | ḍaʿīf | ▫ /dˤaʕiːf/

strong ▪ *[706, adj]*

▪ قَوِيّ ▪ | qawiyy |

necessary ▪ *[707, adj]*

▪ ضَرُورِيّ ▪ | ḍarūriyy |

ready ▪ *[708, adj]*

▪ جَاهِز ▪ | jāhiz |

clean ▪ *[709, adj]*

▪ نَظِيف ▪ | naẓīf |

dirty ▪ *[710, adj]*

▪ قَذِر ▪ | qaḏir |

past ▪ *[711, adj]*

▪ مَاضٍ ▪ | māḍin |

recent ▪ *[712, adj]*

▪ أَخِير ▪ | ʾaḵīr |

present ▪ *[713, adj]*

▪ حَالِيّ ▪ | ḥāliyy |

future ▪ *[714, adj]*

▪ مُسْتَقْبَلِيّ ▪ | mustaqbaliyy |

new ▪ *[715, adj]*

▪ جَدِيد ▪ | jadīd | ▫ /d͡ʒa.diːd/

young ▪ *[716, adj]*

▪ صَغِير ▪ | ṣaḡīr | ▫ /sˤa.ɣiːr/

old ▪ *[717, adj]*

▪ ألسِّنّ كَبِير ▪ | kabīr as-sinn |

ancient ▪ *[718, adj]*

▪ قَدِيم ▪ | qadīm | ▫ /qa.diːm/

modern ▪ *[719, adj]*

▪ عَصْرِيّ ▪ | ʿaṣriyy |

historical ▪ *[720, adj]*

▪ تَارِيخِي ▪ | tārīḵī |

possible ▪ *[722, adj]*

▪ مُمْكِن ▪ | mumkin |

dangerous ▪ *[723, adj]*

▪ خَطِر ▪ | ḵaṭir |

safe ▪ *[724, adj]*

▪ أَمِين ▪ | ʾamīn |

short ▪ *[726, adj]* ▪ *of duration*

- قَصِير - |qaṣīr| □ /qa.sˤiːr/

long • *[727, adj]* • *of duration*

- طَوِيل - |ṭawīl| □ /tˤa.wiːl/

fast • *[728, adj]*

- سَرِيع - |sarī| □ /sa.riːʕ/

slow • *[729, adj]*

- بَطِيء - |baṭī|

previous • *[730, adj]*

- سَابِق - |sābiq| □ /saː.biq/

next • *[731, adj]*

- تَالٍ - |tālin| □ /taː.lin/

last • *[732, adj]*

- آخَر - |ʾāḵar|

female • *[733, adj]*

- أُنْثَى - |ʾunṯā|

male • *[734, adj]*

- ذَكَرِيّ - |ḍakariyy|

married • *[735, adj]*

- مُتَزَوِّج - |mutazawwij|

healthy • *[736, adj]*

- صِحِّيّ - |ṣiḥḥiyy| □ /sˤʕiħ.ħijj/

ill • *[737, adj]*

- مَرِيض - |marīḍ| □ /maˈriːdˤ/

tired • *[738, adj]*

- مُتْعَب - |mutʕab|

pregnant • *[739, adj]*

- حَامِل - |ḥāmil|

hungry • *[740, adj]*

- جَائِع - |jāʾi|

thirsty • *[741, adj]*

- عَطْشَان - |ʿaṭšān|

true. • *[743, adj]* • *concurring with facts*

- صَحِيح - |ṣaḥīḥ|

false. • *[744, adj]*

- زَائِف - |zāʾif|

secret • *[745, adj]*

- سِرِّيّ - |sirriyy|

famous • *[746, adj]*

- مَشْهُور - |mašhūr|

true. • *[747, adj]* • *genuine*

- حَقِيقِيّ - |ḥaqīqiyy|

fake • *[748, adj]*

▪ مســـتعار ▪ |musta'ār|

good ▪ *[749, adj]* ▪ *of evaluation*

▪ حَسَن ▪ |ḥasan|

better ▪ *[750, adj]*

▪ أَفْضَل ▪ |'afḍal|

best ▪ *[751, adj]*

▪ أَفْضَل(اَلـ) ▪ |(al)'afḍal|

perfect ▪ *[752, adj]*

▪ كَامِل ▪ |kāmil| ▫ /ka:.mil/

bad ▪ *[753, adj]* ▪ *of evaluation*

▪ سَيِّئ ▪ |sayyi'| ▫ /saj.ji?/

worst ▪ *[754, adj]*

▪ أَسْوَ (ال) ▪ |(al) 'aswa'|

similar ▪ *[755, adj]*

▪ مُمَاثِل ▪ |mumāṯil|

different ▪ *[756, adj]*

▪ مُخْتَلِف ▪ |muḵtalif|

important ▪ *[757, adj]*

▪ مُهِمّ ▪ |muhimm|

main ▪ *[758, adj]*

▪ رَئِيسِيّ ▪ |ra'īsiyy| ▫ /ra.?i:.sijj/

useful ▪ *[759, adj]*

▪ مُفِيد ▪ |mufīd|

useless ▪ *[760, adj]*

▪ الفائـــدة عـديم ▪ |'adim al-fa'ida|

beautiful ▪ *[761, adj]*

▪ جَمِيل ▪ |jamīl| ▫ /d͡ʒa.mi:l/

nice ▪ *[762, adj]*

▪ حَسَّن ▪ |hassan|

pretty ▪ *[763, adj]*

▪ جَمِيل ▪ |jamīl| ▫ /d͡ʒa.mi:l/

ugly ▪ *[764, adj]*

▪ قَبِيح ▪ |qabīḥ|

right ▪ *[765, adj]*

▪ صَحِيح ▪ |ṣaḥīḥ|

correct ▪ *[766, adj]*

▪ صَحِيح ▪ |ṣaḥīḥ|

wrong ▪ *[767, adj]*

▪ خَطَأ ▪ |ḵaṭa'|

easy ▪ *[768, adj]*

▪ سَهْل ▪ |sahl|

difficult ▪ *[769, adj]*

55

▪ صَعْب ▪ |ṣaʿb|

clever ▪ [770, adj]

▪ ذَكِيّ ▪ |ḍakiyy|

stupid ▪ [771, adj]

▪ غَبِيّ ▪ |ḡabiyy|

good ▪ [772, adj] ▪ of moral

▪ حَسَن ▪ |ḥasan|

bad ▪ [773, adj] ▪ of moral

▪ شَرِير ▪ |šarīr|

certain ▪ [774, adj]

▪ أَكِيد ▪ |ʾakīd|

brave ▪ [775, adj]

▪ شُجَاع ▪ |šujāʿ| ▫ /ʃudʒɑːʕ/

lazy ▪ [776, adj]

▪ كَسْلَان ▪ |kaslān|

kind ▪ [778, adj]

▪ حَنُون ▪ |ḥanūn|

cruel ▪ [779, adj]

▪ قَاسٍ ▪ |qāsin|

polite ▪ [780, adj]

▪ مُؤَدَّب ▪ |muʾaddab|

powerful ▪ [781, adj]

▪ قَوِيّ ▪ |qawiyy|

happy ▪ [782, adj]

▪ سَعِيد ▪ |saʿīd| ▫ /saʕiːd/ ▫ {Egyptian Arabic}

sad ▪ [783, adj]

▪ حَزِين ▪ |ḥazīn|

angry ▪ [784, adj]

▪ غَاضِب ▪ |ḡāḍib| ▫ /ɣaː.dˤib/

funny ▪ [785, adj]

▪ مُضْحِك ▪ |muḍḥik|

interesting ▪ [786, adj]

▪ مُشَوِّق ▪ |mušawwiq|

boring ▪ [787, adj]

▪ مُمِلّ ▪ |mumill|

traditional ▪ [788, adj]

▪ تَقْلِيدِيّ ▪ |taqlīdiyy|

national ▪ [789, adj]

▪ وَطَنِيّ ▪ |waṭaniyy|

foreign ▪ [790, adj]

▪ غَرِيب ▪ |ḡarīb|

private ▪ [791, adj]

56

▪ خَاصّ ▪ |ḵāṣṣ|

public ▪ *[792, adj]*

▪ عَامّ ▪ |ʿāmm| ▫ /ʕaːmm/

rich ▪ *[793, adj]*

▪ غَنِيّ ▪ |ḡaniyy| ▫ /ɣa.nijj/

poor ▪ *[794, adj]*

▪ فَقِير ▪ |faqīr| ▫ /fa.qiːr/

cheap ▪ *[795, adj]*

▪ رَخِيص ▪ |raḵīṣ| ▫ /ra.xiːsˤ/

expensive ▪ *[796, adj]*

▪ غَالٍ ▪ |ḡālin|

why ▪ *[797, adv]*

▪ لِمَاذَا ▪ |limāḏā|

therefore ▪ *[798, adv]*

▪ لِذَلِكَ ▪ |li-ḏālika|

how ▪ *[799, adv]* ▪ *in what state*

▪ كِيـف ▪ |kayf| ▫ /kaj.fa/

how ▪ *[800, adv]* ▪ *to what degree*

▪ كَيْف ▪ |kayf| ▫ /kaj.fa/

most ▪ *[802, adv]*

▪ اَلـ ▫ {a superlative pattern of the adjective} ▪ |al-|

very ▪ *[803, adv]*

▪ جِدًّا ▪ |jiddan| ▫ /d͡ʒid.dan/

even ▪ *[805, adv]*

▪ حَتَّى ▪ |ḥattā|

just ▪ *[806, adv]* ▪ *simply*

▪ فَقَط ▪ |faqaṭ|

only ▪ *[807, adv]*

▪ فَقَط ▪ |faqaṭ|

also ▪ *[808, adv]*

▪ أَيْضًا ▪ |ʾayḍan|

however ▪ *[809, adv]*

▪ لَكِن ▪ |lākin|

where ▪ *[810, adv]* ▪ *direction*

▪ أَيْنَ ىإِلَ ▪ |ʾilā ʾayna|

there ▪ *[811, adv]* ▪ *direction*

▪ هُنَاكَ إِلَى ▪ |ʾilā hunāka|

up ▪ *[812, adv]*

▪ فَوْقَ ▪ |fawqa|

down ▪ *[813, adv]*

▪ تَحْتَ ▪ |taḥta| ▫ /ˈtaħtu/

left ▪ *[816, adv]*

57

	▪ اَلْيَسَار إِلَى ▪ |'ilā l-yasār|
right ▪ [817, adv]	
	▪ اَلْيَمِين إِلَى ▪ |'ilā l-yamīn|
away ▪ [818, adv]	
	▪ بَعِيدًا ▪ |baʿīdan|
somewhere ▪ [820, adv]	
	▪ مَا مَكَان ▪ |makān mā|
nowhere ▪ [821, adv]	
	▪ مَكَان لَا فِي ▪ |fī lā makān|
everywhere ▪ [822, adv]	
	▪ مَكَان كُلّ فِي ▪ |fī kull makān|
here ▪ [823, adv]	
	▪ هُنَا ▪ |hunā| ▫ /hu.naː/
there ▪ [824, adv] ▪ place	
	هُنَاكَ ▪ |hunāka| ▫ /hu.naː.ka/
when ▪ [825, adv]	
	▪ مَتَى ▪ |matā|
then ▪ [826, adv] ▪ at that time	
	▪ آنَذَاكَ ▪ |'ānaḏāka|
ago ▪ [827, adv]	
	▪ قَبْلَ ▪ |qabla|
yesterday ▪ [828, adv]	
	▪ أَمْس ▪ |'ams| ▫ /ʔam.si/
today ▪ [830, adv]	
	▪ اَلْيَوْم ▪ |al-yawm|
now ▪ [831, adv]	
	▪ اَلْآن ▪ |al-'ān| ▫ /al.ʔaː.na/
tomorrow ▪ [832, adv]	
	▪ اَلْغَد ▪ |al-ḡad|
always ▪ [833, adv]	
	▪ دَائِمًا ▪ |dā'iman|
sometimes ▪ [834, adv]	
	▪ أَلْأَحْيَانَ ▪ |'aḥyānan|
ever ▪ [835, adv]	
	▪ يَوْمًا ▪ |yawman|
never ▪ [836, adv]	
	▪ أَبَدًا ▪ |'abadan| ▫ /ʔa.ba.dan/
again ▪ [837, adv]	
	▪ أُخْرَى مَرَّة ▫ <f> ▪ |marra 'uḵrā|
often ▪ [838, adv]	
	▪ كَثِيراً ▪ |kaṯīran| ▫ /ka.θiː.ran/
seldom ▪ [839, adv]	

■ نَادِرًا ■ |nādiran|

daily ▪ *[840, adv]*

■ يَوْمِيًّا ■ |yawmiyyan|

soon ▪ *[841, adv]*

■ قَرِيبًا ■ |qarīban| ▫ /qa.riː.ban/

early ▪ *[842, adv]*

■ مُبَكِّرًا ■ |mubakkiran|

late ▪ *[843, adv]*

■ مُتَأَخِّرًا ■ |muta'ak̲k̲iran|

then ▪ *[844, adv]* ▪ *soon afterward*

■ ثُمَّ ■ |t̲umma| ▫ /θam.ma/

already ▪ *[845, adv]*

■ قَد ■ |qad|

almost ▪ *[846, adv]*

■ تَقْرِيبًا ■ |taqrīban|

still ▪ *[847, adv]*

■ لَا يَزَال ▫ {negative form of زال zaala} ■ |lā yazāl|

maybe ▪ *[848, adv]*

■ رُبَّمَا ■ |rubbamā| ▫ /rub.ba.maː/

how ▪ *[849, adv]* ▪ *in what manner*

■ كَيْف ■ |kayf| ▫ /kaj.fa/

I ▪ *[850, prn]*

■ أَنَا ■ |'anā| ▫ /ʔa.na/

we ▪ *[851, prn]*

■ نَحْنُ ■ |naḥnu| ▫ /naħ.nu/

you ▪ *[852, prn]* ▪ *subject <sg>*

■ أَنْتَ ▫ <m> ■ |'anta| ▫ /ʔanta/

■ أَنْتِ ▫ <f> ■ |'anti| ▫ /ʔanta/

■ أَنْتُمَا ▫ <c du> ■ |'antumā| ▫ /ʔan.tu.maː/

■ أَنْتُم ▫ <m pl> ■ |'antum| ▫ /ʔan.tum/

■ حَضْرَتَك ▫ <m> {formal} ■ |ḥaḍratak|

you ▪ *[853, prn]* ▪ *subject <pl>*

■ أَنْتُمَا ▫ <du> ■ |'antumā| ▫ /ʔan.tu.maː/

■ أَنْتُم ▫ <m pl> ■ |'antum| ▫ /ʔan.tum/

■ أَنْتُنَّ ▫ <f pl> ■ |'antunna| ▫ /ʔan.tun.na/

he ▪ *[854, prn]*

■ هُوَ ■ |huwa| ▫ ['hʊwæ]

she ▪ *[855, prn]*

■ هِيَ ■ |hiya| ▫ /hi.ja/

it ▪ *[856, prn]* ▪ *subjeCT*

■ هُوَ ▫ <m> ■ |huwa| ▫ ['hʊwæ]

■ هِيَ ▫ <f> ■ |hiya| ▫ /hi.ja/

59

they • [857, prn]

- هُمَا ▫ <du> • | humā | ▫ [hʊmæː]
- هُم ▫ <m pl> • | hum | ▫ /hʊm/
- هُنَّ ▫ <f pl> • | hunna | ▫ [ˈhʊnːæ]
- هِيَ ▫ {non-human} • | hiya | ▫ /hi.ja/

me • [858, prn]

- نِي • | -nī |

us • [859, prn]

- نَا • | -nā |

you • [860, prn] • object <sg>

- كَ ▫ <m> • | -ka |
- كِ ▫ <f> • | -ki |
- إِيَّاكَ ▫ <m> • | ʾiyyāka | ▫ /ʔij.jaː.ki/
- إِيَّاكِ ▫ <f> • | ʾiyyāki | ▫ /ʔij.jaː.ki/

you • [861, prn] • object <pl>

- كُم ▫ <m pl> • | -kum |
- كُنَّ ▫ <f pl> • | -kunna |
- كُمَا ▫ <c du> • | -kumā |

him • [862, prn]

- هُ / هِ ▫ <m> • | -hu / -hi |
- إِيَّاهُ ▫ <m> • | ʾiyyāhu |

her • [863, prn]

- هَا • | -hā |
- إِيَّاهَا ▫ <f> • | ʾiyyāhā |

them • [865, prn]

- هُم ▫ <m pl> • | -hum | ▫ /hʊm/
- هُنَّ ▫ <f pl> • | -hunna | ▫ [ˈhʊnːæ]
- هُما ▫ <du> • | -humā | ▫ [hʊmæː]
- إِيَّاهُم ▫ <m pl> • | ʾiyyāhum |
- إِيَّاهُنَّ ▫ <f pl> • | ʾiyyāhunna |
- إِيَّاهُمَا ▫ <du> • | ʾiyyāhumā | ▫ /ʔij.jaː.hu.maː/

everyone • [866, prn]

- الْجَمِيع • | al-jamīʾ |

everything • [867, prn]

- كُلُّه ▫ <m> • | kullahu |
- كُلَّهُم ▫ <pl> • | kullahum |

someone • [868, prn]

- أَحَد • | ʾaḥad | ▫ /ʔa.ħad/

something • [869, prn]

- شَيْء ▫ <m> • | šayʾ |

no one • [870, prn]

60

▪ لَا أَحَد ▪ |lā 'aḥad|

nothing ▪ [871, prn]

▪ لَا شَيْء ▪ |lā šay'|

what ▪ [873, prn]

▪ مَاذَا ▪ |māḏā| ▫ /maː.ðaː/

who ▪ [874, prn]

▪ مَن ▪ |man|

which ▪ [875, prn]

▪ ٱلَّذِي ▪ |allaḏī| ▫ /al.la.ðiː/

that ▪ [876, det]

▪ ذَٰلِكَ ▪ |ḏālika| ▫ /ðaː.li.ka/ ▫ {of pronoun}

this ▪ [877, det]

▪ هَٰذَا ▪ |hāḏā| ▫ /haː.ðaː/ ▫ {of pronoun}

no ▪ [878, det]

▪ لَا ▪ |lā|

every ▪ [879, det]

▪ كُلّ ▪ |kull|

both ▪ [880, det]

▪ كِلَا ▪ |kilā|

same ▪ [881, det]

▪ نَفْسَهُ ▪ |nafsahu|

other ▪ [882, det]

▪ آخَر ▫ <m> ▪ |'āḵar|

such ▪ [883, det]

▪ مِثْل ▪ |miṯl|

my ▪ [884, det]

▪ ي ▫ {suffix, enclitic pronoun} ▪ |-ī|

our ▪ [885, det]

▪ نَا ▪ |-nā|

your ▪ [886, det] ▪ <sg>

▪ ك ▫ {pronunciation differs according to case and level of language formality} ▪ |-k, -ak, -uk|

your ▪ [887, det] ▪ <pl>

▪ كُم ▫ <m> ▪ |-kum|

▪ كُنَّ ▫ <f> ▫ {formal} ▪ |-kunna|

his ▪ [888, det]

▪ هـ ▪ |-hu|

▪ لَهُ ▫ {possessive pronoun} ▪ |lah|

her ▪ [889, det]

▪ هَا ▪ |-hā|

their ▪ [891, det]

▪ لَهُم ▪ |lahum|

61

which ▪ [892, det]

▪ أَيّ ▪ | ʾayy |

few ▪ [893, det]

▪ قَلِيل ▪ | qalīl |

many ▪ [894, det]

▪ كَثِير ▪ | kaṯīr | ▫ /ka.θiːr/

more ▪ [895, det]

▪ أَكْثَر ▪ | ʾakṯar |

enough ▪ [897, det]

▪ كَافٍ ▪ | kāfin |

zero ▪ [899, num]

▪ صِفْر ▫ <m> ▫ {numeral ٠} ▪ | ṣifr |

one ▪ [900, num]

▪ وَاحِد ▪ | wāḥid | ▫ /waː.ḥid/

two ▪ [901, num]

▪ اِثْنَان ▫ {numeral ٢} ▪ | iṯnāni | ▫ /(ʔɪ)θ.naːn/

three ▪ [902, num]

▪ ثَلَاثَة ▫ {numeral ٣} ▪ | ṯalāṯa | ▫ [θaˈlaːθa]

four ▪ [903, num]

▪ أَرْبَعَة ▫ {numeral ٤} ▪ | ʾarbaʿa | ▫ /ʔar.ba.ʕa/

five ▪ [904, num]

▪ خَمْسَة ▫ {numeral ٥} ▪ | ḵamsa | ▫ /xam.sa/

six ▪ [905, num]

▪ سِتَّة ▪ | sitta | ▫ /sit.ta/

seven ▪ [906, num]

▪ سَبْعَة ▫ {numeral ٧} ▪ | sabʿa | ▫ /sab.ʕa/

eight ▪ [907, num]

▪ ثَمَانِيَة ▫ {numeral ٨} ▪ | ṯamāniya | ▫ /θa.maː.ni.ja/

nine ▪ [908, num]

▪ تِسْعَة ▫ {numeral ٩} ▪ | tisʿa | ▫ /tis.ʕa/

ten ▪ [909, num]

▪ عَشَرَة ▫ {numeral ١٠} ▪ | ʿašara | ▫ /ʕa.ʃa.ra/

eleven ▪ [910, num]

▪ عَشَر أَحَد ▫ {numeral - ١١} ▪ | ʾaḥad ʿašar | ▫ /ʔa.ḥa.da ʕa.ʃa.ra/

twelve ▪ [911, num]

▪ عَشَرَ اِثْنَا ▪ | iṯnā ʿašara |

thirteen ▪ [912, num]

▪ عَشَرَ ثَلَاثَ ▫ {numeral ١٣} ▪ | ṯalāṯata ʿašara |

fifteen ▪ [913, num]

▪ عَشَرَ خَمْسَة ▪ | ḵamsata ʿašara |

twenty ▪ [914, num]

• عِشْرِينَ □ {numeral ٢٠} • | ʾišrīna |

thirty • *[915, num]*

• ثَلَاثِينَ □ {numeral - ٣٠} • | talātīna |

fifty • *[916, num]*

• خَمْسِينَ • | kamsīna |

hundred • *[917, num]*

• مِائَة <f> □ {numeral - ١٠٠} • | miʾa |

thousand • *[918, num]*

• أَلْف □ {numeral ١٠٠٠} • | ʾalf | □ /ʔa.lif/

million • *[919, num]*

• مِلْيُون <m> • | milyōn | □ /mil.joːn/

first • *[920, num]*

• أَوَّل • | ʾawwal |

second • *[921, num]*

• ثَانٍ <m> • | tānin |

third • *[922, num]*

• ثَالِث • | tālit |

fifth • *[923, num]*

• خَامِس • | kāmis |

tenth • *[924, num]*

• عَاشِر • | ʾāšir |

and • *[925, cnj]* • *similar words*

• وَ- • | wa- | □ /wɪ/

or • *[927, cnj]*

• أَو • | ʾaw | □ /ʔaw/

• أَم □ {in questions} • | ʾam |

but • *[928, cnj]*

• لٰكِن • | lākin | □ /ˈlaːkin/

although • *[929, cnj]*

• أَنَّ رَغْم • | raḡm ʾanna |

that • *[930, cnj]*

• أَنَّ □ {before subject in the accusative case} • | ʾanna |
□ /ʔan.na/

• إِنَّ □ {after some verbs} • | ʾinna | □ /ʔin/

when • *[931, cnj]* • *at what time*

• مَتَى • | matā |

when • *[932, cnj]* • *at such time*

• عِنْدَمَا • | ʾindamā | □ /ˈʕin.da.maː/

while • *[933, cnj]*

• بَيْنَمَا • | baynamā |

where • *[934, cnj]*

• حَيْثُ • | haytu |

because ▪ *[935, cnj]*

▪ لِأَنَّ ▪ | liʾanna |

so ▪ *[936, cnj]*

▪ فَ ▪ | fa- | ▫ /faːʔ/

if ▪ *[937, cnj]* ▪ *supposing that*

▪ إِنْ ▪ | ʾin | ▫ /ʔin/

unless ▪ *[938, cnj]*

▪ إِلَّا ▪ | ʾillā |

if ▪ *[939, cnj]* ▪ *whether*

▪ إِذَا ▪ | ʾiḏā | ▫ /ʔi.ðan/ ▫ {of adverb}

as ▪ *[940, cnj]*

▪ كَ ▪ | ka |

of ▪ *[941, prp]* ▪ *belonging to*

▪ {genitive construction is used - the thing owned is followed by the owner in the genitive case إِضَافَة | ʾiḏāfa |} ▪

by ▪ *[944, prp]*

▪ مِن قِبَل ▪ | min qibal |

with ▪ *[945, prp]* ▪ *by means of*

▪ بِ ▪ | bi- |

for ▪ *[946, prp]* ▪ *because of*

▪ لِأَجْل ▪ | liʾajl |

for ▪ *[947, prp]* ▪ *intended to*

▪ لِ ▪ | li- | ▫ /li./

about ▪ *[948, prp]* ▪ *concerning*

▪ عَن ▪ | ʿan | ▫ [ʕæn]

than ▪ *[949, prp]*

▪ مِن ▪ | min |

like ▪ *[950, prp]*

▪ مِثْل ▪ | miṯl |

with ▪ *[951, prp]* ▪ *in addition / company*

▪ مَعَ ▪ | maʿa |

without ▪ *[952, prp]*

▪ بِدُونَ ▪ | bi-dūna |

from ▪ *[953, prp]* ▪ *with source*

▪ مِن ▪ | min |

from ▪ *[954, prp]* ▪ *with starting point*

▪ مِن ▪ | min |

to ▪ *[955, prp]* ▪ *direction*

▪ إِلَى ▪ | ʾilā | ▫ /ʔi.laː/

into ▪ *[956, prp]*

▪ دَاخِل ▪ | dāḫil |

against ▪ *[958, prp]* ▪ *direction*

▪ ضِدّ ▪ |ḍidd|

along ▪ *[959, prp]*

▪ طُول عَلَى ▪ |ʿalā ṭūl|

through ▪ *[960, prp]*

▪ خِلَال ▪ |k̠ilāl|

around ▪ *[961, prp]*

▪ حَوْلَ ▪ |ḥawla|

behind ▪ *[962, prp]* ▪ *direction*

▪ وَرَاء ▪ |warāʾ|

at ▪ *[963, prp]* ▪ *place*

▪ عِنْد ▪ |ʿind| ▪ [ˈʕindæ]

in ▪ *[964, prp]* ▪ *contained by*

▪ فِي ▪ |fī| ▪ /fiː/

outside ▪ *[965, prp]*

▪ خَارِج ▪ |k̠ārij| ▪ /xaː.rid͡ʒ/

on ▪ *[966, prp]* ▪ *place*

▪ عَلَى ▪ |ʿalā| ▪ /ʕa.laː/

above ▪ *[967, prp]*

▪ قُفَوْ ▪ |fawqu|

under ▪ *[968, prp]*

▪ تَحْتَ ▪ |taḥta| ▪ /ˈtaħta/

before ▪ *[969, prp]* ▪ *place*

▪ قَبْل ▪ |qabla|

behind ▪ *[970, prp]* ▪ *place*

▪ وَرَاء ▪ |warāʾa|

between ▪ *[971, prp]*

▪ بَيْنَ ▪ |bayna| ▪ /baj.na/

about ▪ *[972, prp]* ▪ *on every side*

▪ وْلَحَ ▪ |ḥawla|

against ▪ *[973, prp]* ▪ *place*

▪ ضِدّ ▪ |ḍidd|

near ▪ *[974, prp]*

▪ مِنَ بِٱلْقُرْب ▪ |bi-l-qurb mina|

at ▪ *[975, prp]* ▪ *time*

▪ فِي ▪ |fī| ▪ /fiː/

on ▪ *[976, prp]* ▪ *date*

▪ عَلَى ▪ |ʿalā| ▪ /ʕa.laː/

during ▪ *[977, prp]*

▪ خِلَال ▪ |k̠ilāla|

in ▪ *[978, prp]* ▪ *after period*

▪ بَعْدَ ▪ |baʿda|

65

since ▪ *[979, prp]*

　　　　　　▪ مُنْذُ ▪ |munḏu|

until ▪ *[980, prp]*

　　　　　　▪ حَتَّى ▪ |ḥattā|

before ▪ *[981, prp]* ▪ *earlier than*

　　　　　　▪ قَبْلَ ▪ |qabla|

after ▪ *[982, prp]* ▪ *later than*

　　　　　　▪ بَعْدَ ▪ |baʻda|

hello ▪ *[983, int]* ▪ *greeting*

　　　　　　▪ عَلَيْكُمُ ٱلسَّلَامُ ▪ |as-salāmu ʻalaykum| ▫ /as.sa.laː.mu ʕa.laj.kum/

hi ▪ *[984, int]*

　　　　　　▪ مَرْحَبًا ▪ |marḥaban| ▫ /mar.ħa.ban/

hello ▪ *[985, int]* ▪ *by telephone*

　　　　　　▪ أَلُو ▪ |ʼālū|

welcome ▪ *[986, int]*

　　　　　　▪ وَسَهْلًا أَهْلًا ▪ |ʼahlan wa-sahlan| ▫ /ʔah.lan wa.sah.lan/

goodbye ▪ *[987, int]*

　　　　　　▪ السَّلَامَة مَعَ ▪ |maʻa s-salāma| ▫ /ma.ʕa‿s.sa.laː.ma/

bye ▪ *[988, int]*

　　　　　　▪ اللِّقَاء إِلَى ▪ |ʼilā l-liqāʼ| ▫ /ʔi.la‿l.li.qaːʔ/

please ▪ *[989, int]*

　　　　　　▪ فَضْلِكَ مِن ▫ {formal, to a man} ▪ |min faḍlika| ▫ /min faḍˤ.li.ka/ ▫ {of adverb}

　　　　　　▪ فَضْلَك مِن {informal, to a man} ▪ |min faḍlak| ▫ /min faḍˤ.li.ka/ ▫ {of adverb}

　　　　　　▪ فَضْلِكِ مِن {formal, to a woman} ▪ |min faḍliki| ▫ /min faḍˤ.li.ka/ ▫ {of adverb}

　　　　　　▪ فَضْلِك مِن {informal, to a woman} ▪ |min faḍlik| ▫ /min faḍˤ.li.ka/ ▫ {of adverb}

thanks ▪ *[990, int]*

　　　　　　▪ شُكْرًا ▪ |šukran| ▫ [ˈʃokrɑn]

you're welcome ▪ *[991, int]*

　　　　　　▪ عَفْوًا ▪ |ʼafwan| ▫ /ʕafwan/

excuse me ▪ *[992, int]*

　　　　　　▪ اِعْذِرْنِي ▪ |iʻḏirnī|

help ▪ *[993, int]*

　　　　　　▪ مُسَاعَدَة ▪ |musāʻada|

cheers ▪ *[994, int]*

　　　　　　▪ صِحَّتِك فِي! ▪ |fī ṣiḥḥatika!|

happy New Year ▪ *[995, int]*

　　　　　　▪ بِخَيْر وَأَنْتُم عَام كُلّ ▪ |kull ʻām waʼantum biḵayr|

yes ▪ *[996, int]*

▪ نَعَم ▪ |naʻam|

no ▪ *[997, int]*

▪ لَا ▪ |lā| ▫ /laː/

OK ▪ *[998, int]*

▪ طَيِّب ▪ |ṭayyib|

well ▪ *[999, int]*

▪ طَيِّب ▪ |ṭayyib|

[ARY] MOROCCAN ARABIC. SURVIVAL DICTIONARY

front • *[016, n]*

■ گدّام • | gəddæm |

light • *[035, n]*

■ ضـو □ <m> ▪ | ḍuw | □ /dˤawː/

fire • *[046, n]*

■ عفْية ▪ | ʕəfya |

water • *[053, n]*

■ ما □ <m> ▪ | mâ |

air • *[055, n]*

■ هُوا □ <m> ▪ | hwa |

paper • *[062, n]*

■ كاغط ▪ | káğiṭ |

gasoline • *[065, n]*

■ ليسـانص □ {l'essence} ▪ | lisanṣ |

place • *[075, n]*

■ بلاصـة □ <f> ▪ | blaṣa |

hour • *[077, n]*

■ ساعة □ <f> ▪ | sa 'a | □ /saːʕa/

minute • *[078, n]*

■ دُقيقة □ <f> ▪ | dqiqa |

day • *[080, n]*

■ يـوم □ <m> ▪ | yum | □ /juːm/

morning • *[083, n]*

■ صْباح □ <m> ▪ | ṣbæḥ |

week • *[085, n]*

■ سـيمانة □ <f> ▪ | simana |

wedding • *[099, n]*

■ عرس □ <m> ▪ | 3rs |

end • *[103, n]*

■ خر □ <m> ▪ | ḵar |

clock • *[104, n]*

■ انـةكّـم □ <f> ▪ | magana | □ /ma.gaː.na/

moon • *[107, n]*

■ گمـرة □ <f> ▪ | gemra |

fog • *[112, n]*

■ ضْبابة □ <f> ▪ | ḍbæba |

rain • *[113, n]*

■ شْتا ▪ | šta |

snow • *[114, n]*

■ تلْج □ <m> ▪ | telj |

wind ▪ *[115, n]*

    ▪ بَرْد □ <m> ▪ |bərd|

mountain ▪ *[122, n]*

    ▪ جْبَل □ <m> ▪ |jbəl|

street ▪ *[135, n]*

    ▪ زنقــة ▪ |zanqa|

bridge ▪ *[137, n]*

    ▪ قنطــرة □ <f> ▪ |qənṭra| □ /qantˤra/

house ▪ *[140, n]*

    ▪ دار □ <f> ▪ |dar| □ /daːr/

roof ▪ *[144, n]*

    ▪ ســقف □ <m> ▪ |sqaf|

wall ▪ *[145, n]*

    ▪ حيــط □ <m> ▪ |ḥəyṭ| □ /ħiːtˤ/

door ▪ *[148, n]*

    ▪ بــاب □ <m> ▪ |bāb| □ /baːb/

window ▪ *[149, n]*

    ▪ شـرجم □ <m> ▪ |šəržəm| □ /ʃar.ʒam/

kitchen ▪ *[153, n]*

    ▪ كوزينـــة ▪ |kuzina|

hotel ▪ *[156, n]*

    ▪ أوطيــل □ <m> ▪ |ʼoṭil|

chair ▪ *[157, n]*

    ▪ كرْسي □ <m> ▪ |kərsi|

bed ▪ *[158, n]*

    ▪ ناموسيّة □ <f> ▪ |nāmūsiyya|

table ▪ *[160, n]*

    ▪ طبْلة □ <f> ▪ |ṭəbla|

mirror ▪ *[162, n]*

    ▪ مرُاية □ <f> ▪ |mræya|

carpet ▪ *[163, n]*

    ▪ زربيـــة □ <f> ▪ |zarbiya|

blanket ▪ *[164, n]*

    ▪ بَطَّانيَّة ▪ |baṭṭāniyya|

curtain ▪ *[167, n]*

    ▪ خميـة □ <f> ▪ |ḵamiyya|

fork ▪ *[172, n]*

    ▪ فرشــــيطة ▪ |furšeyṭa|

knife ▪ *[173, n]*

    ▪ موس ▪ |muus| □ /muːs/

box ▪ *[177, n]*

    ▪ صنْدوقة □ <f> ▪ |ṣənduqa|

bag • *[178, n]*

■ خنشـة <f> ■ |ḵenša| ■ /χan.ʃa/

battery • *[180, n]*

■ بــاتري ■ |bātrī|

oven • *[184, n]*

■ فرّان <m> ■ |farrān|

tap • *[186, n]*

■ روبيـــني ■ |rūbīnī|

bicycle • *[198, n]*

■ بشـــكليت ■ |bešklīt|

boat • *[200, n]*

■ فلوكـة ■ |felūka|

shirt • *[210, n]*

■ قميجـة <f> ■ |qəmiǧa|

sweater • *[211, n]*

■ تـــريكو ■ |trīkū|

shoe • *[217, n]*

■ سبّاط <m> ■ |sebbaṬ|

grass • *[223, n]*

■ ربيـــع <m> ■ |rbiʕ| ■ /rbiːʕ/

cat • *[228, n]*

■ مش ■ |mešš| ■ /muʃː/

horse • *[230, n]*

■ عَوْد ■ |ʕawd|

sheep • *[231, n]*

■ غْنم <f> ■ |ghnem|

pig • *[232, n]*

■ حلـوف ■ |ḥalūf|

cow • *[233, n]*

■ بَڭْرة <f> ■ |bəgra|

monkey • *[238, n]*

■ قِرْد <m> ■ |qərd|

frog • *[240, n]*

■ جرانـا <m> ■ |žrana|

bird • *[241, n]*

■ برطـال ■ |bərṭāl|

fish • *[244, n]*

■ حُوت <m> ■ |ḥut| ■ /ħuːt/

body • *[247, n]*

■ دات <m> ■ |dæt|

head • *[251, n]*

■ رأس <m> ■ |ras|

arm ▪ [255, n]

▪ يـد ▫ <m> ▪ |id|

skin ▪ [262, n]

▪ جلـد ▫ <m> ▪ |jəld|

health ▪ [265, n]

▪ صْحة ▫ <f> ▪ |ṣḥa|

hospital ▪ [271, n]

▪ صـــبيطار ▫ <m> ▪ |ṣbiṭar|

cigarette ▪ [273, n]

▪ روݣ ▪ |garro|

face ▪ [274, n]

▪ وَجْه ▫ <m> ▪ |wejh|

eye ▪ [275, n]

▪ عيـن ▫ <m pl> ▪ |ˈein|

nose ▪ [277, n]

▪ نيـف ▫ <m> ▪ |nīf| ▫ /ni:f/

mouth ▪ [278, n]

▪ فـم ▪ |fumm|

food ▪ [280, n]

▪ ماكلـة ▫ <f> ▪ |makla|

breakfast ▪ [281, n]

▪ فطـور ▫ <m> ▪ |fṭur|

onion ▪ [288, n]

▪ بصـــلة ▫ <f> ▪ |beṣla|

tomato ▪ [289, n]

▪ ماطيشـة ▫ <f> ▪ |maṭīša| ▫ /ma.tˤi:.ʃa/

potato ▪ [290, n]

▪ بْطاطا ▫ <f> ▪ |bṭæṭa|

orange ▪ [292, n]

▪ ليمـون ▫ <m> ▪ |limun|

bread ▪ [296, n]

▪ خـبز ▫ {North} ▪ |ḵubz|

cheese ▪ [297, n]

▪ فرومـاج ▪ |fromæž|

sausage ▪ [301, n]

▪ سوســيس ▪ |susis|

restaurant ▪ [312, n]

▪ ريسـطورة ▫ <f> ▪ |risṭora|

book ▪ [328, n]

▪ كتـاب ▫ <m> ▪ |ktab|

pen ▪ [333, n]

▪ ســـتيلو ▪ |stilu| ▫ /stilu/ ▫ {of adverb}

71

name ▪ *[337, n]*

▪ سْمِيّة ▫ <f> ▫ {becoming سْميت |smit|, when affixed} ▪ |sməyya|

message ▪ *[346, n]*

▪ ميساج ▫ |misaž|

girl ▪ *[356, n]*

▪ بنـت ▫ <f> ▪ |bent|

woman ▪ *[357, n]*

▪ مرا ▫ <f> ▪ |mrâ| ▫ /mra/

daughter ▪ *[363, n]*

▪ بنـت ▫ <f> ▪ |bent|

guest ▪ *[371, n]*

▪ ضِيف ▫ <m> ▪ |ḍif| ▫ /dˤi:f/

drum ▪ *[385, n]*

▪ طبـل ▫ <m> ▪ |ṭbel|

money ▪ *[401, n]*

▪ فلــوس ▫ <m pl> ▪ |flus| ▫ /fluːs \ fal.luːs/ ▫ {one may be incorrect}

salary ▪ *[404, n]*

▪ اجرة ▫ <f> ▪ |ejra|

shop ▪ *[410, n]*

▪ حـانوت ▫ <m> ▪ |ḥanut|

factory ▪ *[413, n]*

▪ لُزين ▫ <m> ▪ |lŭzīn|

farm ▪ *[415, n]*

▪ فرمـة ▫ <f> ▪ |ferma|

farmer ▪ *[416, n]*

▪ فـلاح ▫ <m> ▪ |fellaḥ|

tool ▪ *[417, n]*

▪ زاند ▫ <m pl> ▪ |dezan|

key ▪ *[420, n]*

▪ سـاروت ▫ <f> ▪ |særut|

prison ▪ *[431, n]*

▪ حْبْس ▫ <m> ▪ |ḥəbs|

dance ▪ *[445, n]*

▪ شـطح ▫ |šṭeḥ|

die ▪ *[457, v]*

▪ مات ▫ |māt|

change ▪ *[463, v]* ▪ *to make into different*

▪ بذّل ▫ |bəddəl|

open ▪ *[471, v]*

▪ حل ▫ |ḥəll|

72

measure ▪ *[473, v]*
▪ عــبر ▪ |ʕbər|

arrive ▪ *[487, v]*
▪ وْصل ▪ |wṣəl|

enter ▪ *[488, v]*
▪ دخل ▪ |dkhel|

run ▪ *[492, v]*
▪ جْرى ▪ |jra| ▫ /ʒra/

pull ▪ *[498, v]*
▪ جر ▪ |jerr|

bring ▪ *[515, v]*
▪ جاب ▪ |ğab|

lose ▪ *[519, v]* ▪ *to cease possesion*
▪ وذَر ▪ |wəddər|

finish ▪ *[537, v]*
▪ كمّل ▪ |kammal|

wait ▪ *[539, v]*
▪ تْسنّى ▪ |tsənna|

wear ▪ *[543, v]*
▪ لْبس ▪ |lbəs|

cough ▪ *[545, v]*
▪ كحـب ▪ |kḥab|

kiss ▪ *[546, v]*
▪ بَاس ▪ |bas| ▫ /baːs/

drink ▪ *[552, v]*
▪ شْرب ▪ |shreb| ▫ /ʃrab/

cook ▪ *[554, v]*
▪ طيـب ▪ |ṭeyyeb| ▫ /tˤaj.jib/

sleep ▪ *[555, v]*
▪ نعـس ▪ |neʕs|

look ▪ *[558, v]*
▪ شـاف ▪ |šaf| ▫ /ʃaːf/

see ▪ *[559, v]*
▪ شـاف ▪ |šaf| ▫ /ʃaːf/

hear ▪ *[561, v]*
▪ سْمع ▪ |sməʕ| ▫ /smaʕ/

find ▪ *[565, v]*
▪ لقـى ▪ |lqa|

remember ▪ *[570, v]* ▪ *to recall*
▪ عُقْل ▪ |ˈqəl|

forget ▪ *[572, v]*
▪ نْسى ▪ |nsa| ▫ /nsa \ nas.sa/ ▫ {one may be incorrect}

understand ▪ [573, v]

  ▪ فهـم ▪ |fhem|

believe ▪ [576, v]

  ▪ تـاق ▪ |taq| ▫ /taːq/

translate ▪ [588, v]

  ▪ ترْجم ▪ |tərjəm|

fear ▪ [594, v]

  ▪ خاف ▪ |xæf|

want ▪ [598, v]

  ▪ حب ▪ |ḥabb|

speak ▪ [607, v]

  ▪ هُدر ▪

say ▪ [608, v]

  ▪ الكَ North ▪ |gæl|

teach ▪ [638, v]

  ▪ قرّى ▪ |qerra|

learn ▪ [639, v]

  ▪ تُعلّم ▪ |t3əlləm|

sell ▪ [640, v]

  ▪ بـاع ▪ |bāʼ|

buy ▪ [641, v]

  ▪ شـرى ▪ |šra|

pay ▪ [642, v]

  ▪ خلّص ▪ |ḳəlləṣ| ▫ /χal.lasˤ/

dance ▪ [648, v]

  ▪ شـطح ▪ |šṭeḥ|

full ▪ [661, adj] ▪ containing maximum

  ▪ عامر ▫ <m> ▪ |ʕamər|

long ▪ [666, adj] ▪ of size

  ▪ طويـل ▪ |ṭwil|

narrow ▪ [669, adj]

  ▪ مضـيق ▫ <m> ▪ |mḍayyaq|

wide ▪ [670, adj]

  ▪ عـريض ▪ |ʼariḍ|

heavy ▪ [674, adj]

  ▪ ثُقيل ▪ |tqil|

black ▪ [678, adj]

  ▪ كحـال ▪ |kḥāl|

wet ▪ [691, adj]

  ▪ لثُفـاز ▫ <m> ▪ |fāzag|

hard ▪ [692, adj]

  ▪ قاصـح ▪ |qāṣḥ|

weak ▪ *[705, adj]*

▪ عيّان ▫ <m> ▪ |ʕəyyæn| ▫ /ʕij.jaːn/

dirty ▪ *[710, adj]*

▪ موسخ ▪ |musək̲| ▫ /muːs.sax/

bad ▪ *[753, adj]* ▪ *of evaluation*

▪ خْيب ▪ |k̲æyb|

beautiful ▪ *[761, adj]*

▪ زوين ▪ |zwin|

ugly ▪ *[764, adj]*

▪ خيب ▪ |k̲əyb|

difficult ▪ *[769, adj]*

▪ واعر ▪ |wa 'r| ▫ /waːʕɪr/

clever ▪ *[770, adj]*

▪ مطور ▫ <m> ▪ |mṭəwwər|

kind ▪ *[778, adj]*

▪ ضـريف ▪ |ḍrīf|

cheap ▪ *[795, adj]*

▪ رْخيص ▪ |rk̲iṣ|

why ▪ *[797, adv]*

▪ غلاش ▪ |ʕlæš| ▫ /ʕlaːʃ/

however ▪ *[809, adv]*

▪ شـي هد وخى ▪ |wak̲a had ši|

somewhere ▪ *[820, adv]*

▪ موضع فشـي ▪ |faši muḍa3|

today ▪ *[830, adv]*

▪ ليـوم ▪ |lyom|

now ▪ *[831, adv]*

▪ دبـا ▪ |dæba|

often ▪ *[838, adv]*

▪ ديما ▪ |dima|

early ▪ *[842, adv]*

▪ بكـري ▪ |bakri|

how ▪ *[849, adv]* ▪ *in what manner*

▪ كيفـاش ▪ |kifāš|

I ▪ *[850, prn]*

▪ انـا ▫ <m/f> ▪ |æna|

no one ▪ *[870, prn]*

▪ واحد حتّا ▫ <m> ▪ |ḥətta wæḥed|

nothing ▪ *[871, prn]*

▪ والـو ▪ |wælu| ▫ /waːlu/ {of noun}

what ▪ *[873, prn]*

▪ اشـنو Saudi ▪ |ʾašnū|

who ▪ *[874, prn]*

　　　　　　　▪ شــكون ▪ |škun| ▫ /ʃkuːn/

that ▪ *[876, det]*

　　　　　　　▪ هدك ▫ <m/f> ▪ |hədək|

this ▪ *[877, det]*

　　　　　　　▪ هـ ▪ |həd|

our ▪ *[885, det]*

　　　　　　　▪ ـنا ▪ |na|

your ▪ *[887, det]* ▪ <pl>

　　　　　　　▪ ـكم ▫ <m/f> ▪ |kəm|

two ▪ *[901, num]*

　　　　　　　▪ جُوج ▪ |žūž| ▫ /ʒuːʒ/

three ▪ *[902, num]*

　　　　　　　▪ ثْلاتة ▪ |tlata| ▫ /tlaː.ta/

while ▪ *[933, cnj]*

　　　　　　　▪ فْلُوقْط ▪ |fəlwəqt|

because ▪ *[935, cnj]*

　　　　　　　▪ حيـت ▪ |Hit| ▫ /ħiːt/

if ▪ *[937, cnj]* ▪ *supposing that*

　　　　　　　▪ كان كون ▪ |kon kan|

if ▪ *[939, cnj]* ▪ *whether*

　　　　　　　▪ إلى ▪ |ila|

with ▪ *[945, prp]* ▪ *by means of*

　　　　　　　▪ بْ ▪ |b-|

with ▪ *[951, prp]* ▪ *in addition / company*

　　　　　　　▪ مْع ▪ |m 'ə|

without ▪ *[952, prp]*

　　　　　　　▪ بْلى ▪ |bla|

in ▪ *[964, prp]* ▪ *contained by*

　　　　　　　▪ فـي ▪ |fi|

　　　　　　　▪ فـ ▫ {agglutinated} ▪ |fi|

before ▪ *[969, prp]* ▪ *place*

　　　　　　　▪ گّدَّام ▪ |gəddæm|

since ▪ *[979, prp]*

　　　　　　　▪ من ▪ |mən|

before ▪ *[981, prp]* ▪ *earlier than*

　　　　　　　▪ گُبَل ▪ |gbəl|

hi ▪ *[984, int]*

　　　　　　　▪ السـلام ▪ |s-salām|

welcome ▪ *[986, int]*

　　　　　　　▪ مرحبـة ▪ |marḥaba|

goodbye ▪ *[987, int]*

▪ بْسْلَامَة | bslāma |

please ▪ *[989, int]*

▪ عفـك ▪ |'æfək|

cheers ▪ *[994, int]*

▪ والعافيـــة بالصـــحة ▪ | saha wa'afiab |

[ARZ] EGYPTIAN ARABIC. SURVIVAL DICTIONARY

thing ▪ *[001, n]*

▪ شيء □ <m> ▪ |šeʾ|

part ▪ *[003, n]*

▪ جزء □ <m> ▪ |guzʔ|

half ▪ *[004, n]*

▪ نص □ <m> ▪ |nuṣ|

pair ▪ *[007, n]*

▪ جوز □ <m> ▪ |gōz|

side ▪ *[013, n]*

▪ جنب □ <m> ▪ |ganb|

front ▪ *[016, n]*

▪ قدام □ <m> ▪ |ʔudaam|

circle ▪ *[020, n]*

▪ ديرة □ <f> ▪ |dayira|

metre ▪ *[030, n]*

▪ متر □ <m> ▪ |metr|

litre ▪ *[032, n]*

▪ لتر □ <m> ▪ |letr|

kilogram ▪ *[034, n]*

▪ كيلوجرام □ <m> ▪ |kilogrām|

light ▪ *[035, n]*

▪ نور □ <m> ▪ |nor|

sound ▪ *[037, n]*

▪ صوت □ <m> ▪ |ṣot| □ /sˤoːt/

dust ▪ *[045, n]*

▪ تراب □ <m> ▪ |turāb|

fire ▪ *[046, n]*

▪ نار ▪ |nar|

gold ▪ *[050, n]*

▪ دهب □ <m> ▪ |dahab|

silver ▪ *[052, n]*

▪ فضة □ <f> ▪ |faḍa|

water ▪ *[053, n]*

▪ مية ▪ |máyya| □ /ˈmæjːæ/

ice ▪ *[054, n]*

▪ تلج □ <m> ▪ |talg|

air ▪ *[055, n]*

▪ هوا □ <m> ▪ |hawa| □ /ˈhawɑ/

sand ▪ *[056, n]*

▪ رمل □ <m> ▪ |raml|

stone ▪ [057, n]

▪ حجر ◦ <m> ▪ | ḥagar |

glass ▪ [059, n] ▪ substance

▪ قـزاز ◦ <m> ▪ | ˈezāz | ◦ [ʔeˈzæːz]

paper ▪ [062, n]

▪ ورق ◦ <m> ▪ | wáraʼ |

soap ▪ [067, n]

▪ صـــابونة ◦ <f> ▪ | ṣabūna |

step ▪ [069, n]

▪ خطوة ◦ <f> ▪ | ḫaṭwa |

north ▪ [072, n]

▪ شـمال ◦ <m> ▪ | shamal |

south ▪ [073, n]

▪ جنـوب ◦ <m> ▪ | ganūb |

west ▪ [074, n]

▪ غرب ◦ <m> ▪ | ġarb |

place ▪ [075, n]

▪ مكان ◦ <m> ▪ | makān |

time ▪ [076, n] ▪ passing of events

▪ وقـت ◦ <m> ▪ | waʔt |

hour ▪ [077, n]

▪ ساعة ◦ <f> ▪ | saˈa | ◦ /ˈseʕɑ/

second ▪ [079, n]

▪ يـتّــان ◦ <f> ▪ | sanya |

day ▪ [080, n]

▪ يـوم ◦ <m> ▪ | yoom |

evening ▪ [082, n]

▪ ليـل ▪ | lel |

night ▪ [084, n]

▪ ليـل ◦ <m> ▪ | lel |

week ▪ [085, n]

▪ اسـبوع ◦ <m> ▪ | ˈesboʻ |

year ▪ [086, n]

▪ سـنة ◦ <f> ▪ | sana |

month ▪ [087, n]

▪ شـهر ◦ <m> ▪ | šahr |

season ▪ [088, n]

▪ فصـل ◦ <m> ▪ | faṣl |

spring ▪ [090, n]

▪ ربيـع ▪ | rabiiʕ |

summer ▪ [091, n]

▪ صـيف ◦ <m> ▪ | ṣef |

79

winter • *[092, n]*

■ شِـــتا ▫ <m> ■ |šeta|

age • *[094, n]*

■ عمر ▫ <m> ■ |ʿumr|

birthday • *[098, n]*

■ ميـلاد عيـد ▫ <m> ■ |ʿīd melad|

end • *[103, n]*

■ نهايـة ▫ <f> ■ |nehaya|

clock • *[104, n]*

■ ساعة ▫ <f> ■ |sāʿa| ▫ /ˈseʕɑ/

star • *[106, n]*

■ نجمة ▫ <f> ■ |negma|

moon • *[107, n]*

■ قمـر ▫ <m> ■ |ʾamar|

sun • *[108, n]*

■ شمـس ▫ <f> ■ |šams|

sky • *[109, n]*

■ سماء ▫ <f> ■ |sama|

cloud • *[111, n]*

■ ســحابة ▫ <f> ■ |saḥāba|

fog • *[112, n]*

■ شـــبورة ▫ <m> ■ |šabbūra|

rain • *[113, n]*

■ مطر ▫ <m> ■ |maṭar|

snow • *[114, n]*

■ تلــج ▫ <m> ■ |talg|

lake • *[117, n]*

■ بُحَيْرَة ▫ <f> ■ |buḥayra|

river • *[118, n]*

■ نهر ▫ <m> ■ |nahr|

hill • *[121, n]*

■ تـل ▫ <m> ■ |tall|

mountain • *[122, n]*

■ جبــل ▫ <m> ■ |gabal|

cave • *[123, n]*

■ كهف ▫ <m> ■ |kahf|

country • *[125, n]*

■ بلــد ▫ <f> ■ |balad|

island • *[127, n]*

■ جــزيرة ▫ <f> ■ |gezīra|

desert • *[128, n]*

■ صـحرة ▫ <f> ■ |ṣaḥara|

forest ▪ *[129, n]*

▪ غابـة ◦ <f> ▪ |ḡāba|

city ▪ *[130, n]*

▪ مدينـة ◦ |madīna|

town ▪ *[131, n]*

▪ مدينـة ◦ <f> ▪ |madina|

village ▪ *[132, n]*

▪ قريـة ◦ <f> ▪ |qarya|

road ▪ *[134, n]*

▪ طـريق ◦ <m> ▪ |tariʾ|

bridge ▪ *[137, n]*

▪ كوبـري ◦ <m> ▪ |kobri|

building ▪ *[139, n]*

▪ ةعمار ◦ <f> ▪ |ʿimāra|

house ▪ *[140, n]*

▪ بيـت ◦ <m> ▪ |bēt|

station ▪ *[141, n]*

▪ محطة ◦ <f> ▪ |maḥaṭa|

airport ▪ *[142, n]*

▪ مطار ▪ |maṭār|

roof ▪ *[144, n]*

▪ سـطح ◦ <m> ▪ |saTH|

door ▪ *[148, n]*

▪ بـاب ◦ <m> ▪ |bāb| ◦ /bɛːp/

window ▪ *[149, n]*

▪ شـباك ◦ <m> ▪ |šebbāk, šobbāk|

room ▪ *[151, n]*

▪ أوضة ◦ <f> ▪ |ʾōḍa| ◦ [ʔoːdˤɑ]

kitchen ▪ *[153, n]*

▪ مطبـخ ◦ <m> ▪ |maṭbaḵ|

hotel ▪ *[156, n]*

▪ فُنْدُق ◦ <m> ▪ |fundoʾ|

chair ▪ *[157, n]*

▪ كرسـي ◦ <m> ▪ |kursī|

bed ▪ *[158, n]*

▪ سـرير ◦ <m> ▪ |serīr|

table ▪ *[160, n]*

▪ تربــيزة ◦ <f> ▪ |ṭárabēza| ◦ [tɑrɑˈbeːzɑ]

mirror ▪ *[162, n]*

▪ مرايـة ◦ <f> ▪ |mirāya|

carpet ▪ *[163, n]*

▪ سـجادة ◦ <f> ▪ |segada|

81

towel • *[166, n]*

■ فوطـة □ <f> ■ |fūṭa|

curtain • *[167, n]*

ســتارة □ <f> ■ |setāra|

pot • *[168, n]*

■ حلـة □ <f> ■ |ḥala|

cup • *[169, n]*

فنجــان □ <m> ■ |fengān|

glass • *[170, n]* • ***vessel***

■ كبايــة □ <f> ■ |kubaya|

plate • *[171, n]*

■ طبـق □ <m> ■ |ṭabaq|

fork • *[172, n]*

■ شـوكة □ <f> ■ |šōka|

knife • *[173, n]*

■ ســكينة □ <f> ■ |sikkīna|

spoon • *[174, n]*

 قـةمعل □ <f> ■ |ma'lá'a|

bottle • *[176, n]*

■ قـزازة □ <f> ■ |'ezāza|

bag • *[178, n]*

■ كيســة □ <f> ■ |kisa|

machine • *[179, n]*

■ آلـة □ <f> ■ |'āla|

battery • *[180, n]*

■ بطاريــة □ <m> ■ |baṭāreya|

car • *[196, n]*

عَرَبِيَّة □ <f> ■ |'arabiyya|

bicycle • *[198, n]*

■ عجلـة □ <f> ■ |'agala|

boat • *[200, n]*

■ مركب □ <m> ■ |markeb|

driver • *[203, n]*

■ سـواق □ <m> ■ |sawwā'|

pants • *[212, n]*

■ بنطلـون □ <m> ■ |banṭalūn|

skirt • *[213, n]*

■ جيبــة □ <f> ■ |žība| □ [ʒi:ba]

hat • *[215, n]*

■ برنيتــة □ <f> ■ |burnēta|

boot • *[216, n]*

■ بـوت □ <m> ■ |boot|

shoe ▪ [217, n]

▪ جزمة ▫ <f> ▪ |gazma| ▫ [gæz'mæ]

umbrella ▪ [219, n]

▪ شمسـية ▫ <f> ▪ |šamseya|

mushroom ▪ [222, n]

▪ مشروم ▫ <m> ▪ |mášrom, mašrūm|

grass ▪ [223, n]

▪ نجيلـة ▪ |negila|

tree ▪ [224, n]

▪ شـجرة ▫ <f> ▪ |šagara or sagara|

flower ▪ [226, n]

▪ وردة ▫ <f> ▪ |warda|

animal ▪ [227, n]

▪ حيـوان ▫ <m> ▪ |ḥayawan|

cat ▪ [228, n]

▪ قـط ▫ <m> ▪ |'uṭṭ| ▫ /ʔʊtˤ:/

dog ▪ [229, n]

▪ كلـب ▫ <m> ▪ |kalb|

horse ▪ [230, n]

▪ حصـان ▫ <m> ▪ |ḥuṣān|

sheep ▪ [231, n]

▪ خروف ▫ <m> ▪ |xarūf|

pig ▪ [232, n]

▪ خـنزير ▫ <m> ▪ |xanzīr|

cow ▪ [233, n]

▪ بقـرة ▫ <f> ▪ |baʾara|

lion ▪ [234, n]

▪ سـبع ▫ <m> ▪ |sabʿ| ▫ [ˈsæbʕ]

elephant ▪ [236, n]

▪ فيـل ▫ <m> ▪ |fiil|

mouse ▪ [237, n]

▪ فـار ▪ |fār|

monkey ▪ [238, n]

▪ نسـناس ▫ <m> ▪ |nesnās|

snake ▪ [239, n]

▪ تعبـان ▫ <m> ▪ |tiʿbān|

frog ▪ [240, n]

▪ ضـفدع ▫ <m> ▪ |ḍufḍaʿ|

bird ▪ [241, n]

▪ طـير ▫ <m> ▪ |ṭēr|

chicken ▪ [242, n]

▪ فرخـة ▫ <f> ▪ |farxa|

duck • *[243, n]*
■ بطــة □ <f> ■ |baṭa|

fish • *[244, n]*
■ سَمَكَة □ <f> ■ |sámaka|

insect • *[245, n]*
■ حشـرة □ <f> ■ |ḥašara|

body • *[247, n]*
■ جسـم □ <m> ■ |gesm|

back • *[248, n]* • *of body*
■ ضهر □ <m> ■ |ḍahr|

belly • *[249, n]*
■ بطــن □ <f> ■ |baṭn|

chest • *[250, n]*
■ صـدر □ <m> ■ |sedr|

head • *[251, n]*
■ راس □ <f> ■ |ras| □ [rɑːs]

neck • *[252, n]*
■ رقبــة □ <f> ■ |raʔaba|

foot • *[253, n]* • *of body*
■ رجل □ <f> ■ |regl|

leg • *[254, n]*
■ رجل □ <f> ■ |regl|

arm • *[255, n]*
■ دراع □ <m> ■ |derāʿ|

hand • *[257, n]*
■ إيـد □ <f> ■ |'iid|

blood • *[258, n]*
■ دم □ <m> ■ |dam|

heart • *[259, n]*
■ قلــب □ <m> ■ |'alb| □ /ʔælb/

brain • *[260, n]*
■ مخ □ <m> ■ |muxx|

stomach • *[261, n]*
■ معدة □ <f> ■ |meʿda|

skin • *[262, n]*
■ جلـد □ <m> ■ |gild| □ [geld]

bone • *[263, n]*
■ عضـم □ <m> ■ |ʕadm|

tooth • *[264, n]*
■ سـن □ <m> ■ |senn|

health • *[265, n]*
■ صـحة □ <f> ■ |ṣeḥa|

doctor ▪ *[272, n]*

▪ دكتـــور ▫ <m> ▪ |doktōr|

face ▪ *[274, n]*

▪ وِشّ ▫ <m> ▪ |weš|

eye ▪ *[275, n]*

▪ عيــن ▫ <f> ▪ |ʿén|

ear ▪ *[276, n]*

▪ ودن ▫ <m> ▪ |widn|

nose ▪ *[277, n]*

▪ منـاخير ▫ <f> ▪ |manaḵīr| ▫ [mænæˈxiːr]

mouth ▪ *[278, n]*

▪ بـق ▪ |boʿ|

hair ▪ *[279, n]*

▪ شـعرة ▪ |šaʿra|

breakfast ▪ *[281, n]*

▪ فطـار ▫ <m> ▪ |feṭār|

dinner ▪ *[283, n]*

▪ عشـا ▪ |ʿáša|

sandwich ▪ *[286, n]*

▪ ســـندويتش ▫ <m> ▪ |sandawetš|

onion ▪ *[288, n]*

▪ بصــلة ▫ <f> ▪ |baṣala|

tomato ▪ *[289, n]*

▪ طمطمايـة ▫ <f> ▪ |ṭamaṭmaya|

potato ▪ *[290, n]*

▪ بطـاطس ▫ <f> ▪ |baṭáṭes|

apple ▪ *[291, n]*

▪ تفاحـــة ▫ <f> ▪ |tuffāḥa|

orange ▪ *[292, n]*

▪ برتقــان ▫ <col> ▪ |burtuʾān|
▪ برتقانـــة ▫ <f sgv> ▪ |burtuʾāna|

grape ▪ *[293, n]*

▪ عنـب ▫ <m> ▪ |ʿenab|

rice ▪ *[295, n]*

▪ رزة ▫ <f> ▪ |ruza|

bread ▪ *[296, n]*

▪ عيـش ▫ <m> ▪ |ʿéš|

cheese ▪ *[297, n]*

▪ جبنـة ▫ <f> ▪ |gebna|

milk ▪ *[298, n]*

▪ لبــن ▫ <m> ▪ |laban|

meat ▪ *[300, n]*

▪ لحمة ▫ <f> ▪ |láḥma|

***sausage* ▪ [301, n]**

▪ سجق ▫ <m> ▪ |suguʾ|

***cake* ▪ [302, n]**

▪ كيك ▫ <m pl> ▪ |kek|

***sauce* ▪ [305, n]**

▪ صوص ▫ <m> ▪ |ṣoṣ|

***spice* ▪ [306, n]**

▪ توابل ▫ <f pl> ▪ |tawabel|

***salt* ▪ [307, n]**

▪ ملح ▫ <m> ▪ |malḥ|

***coffee* ▪ [308, n]**

▪ قَهْوَة ▫ <f> ▪ |ʾahwa|

***beer* ▪ [310, n]**

▪ بيرة ▫ <f> ▪ |bīra| ▫ [biːra]

***wine* ▪ [311, n]**

▪ نبيت ▫ <m> ▪ |nibiit| ▫ [nebiːt]

***dream* ▪ [313, n]**

▪ حلم ▫ <m> ▪ |ḥelm|

***information* ▪ [315, n]**

▪ معلومة ▫ <f> ▪ |maʿluma|

***news* ▪ [316, n]**

▪ خَبَر ▫ <m> ▪ |ḵabar|

***mind* ▪ [318, n]**

▪ عقل ▫ <m> ▪ |ʕaʔl|

number* ▪ [324, n] ▪ *of rank

▪ نمره ▫ <f> ▪ |nímra|

***book* ▪ [328, n]**

▪ كتاب ▫ <m> ▪ |ketæb|

***page* ▪ [331, n]**

▪ صفحة ▫ <f> ▪ |ṣafḥa|

***pen* ▪ [333, n]**

▪ قلم ▫ <m> ▪ |ʾalam|

***name* ▪ [337, n]**

▪ اسم ▫ <m> ▪ |esm|

***word* ▪ [338, n]**

▪ كلمة ▫ <f> ▪ |kilma|

***sentence* ▪ [339, n]**

▪ جملة ▫ <f> ▪ |gumla|

***language* ▪ [340, n]**

▪ لغة ▫ <f> ▪ |loḡa|

***voice* ▪ [345, n]**

■ صوت □ <m> ▪ |ṣowt| □ /sˤoːt/

culture ▪ *[349, n]*

■ ثقافـــة □ <f> ▪ |saqāfa, ṯaqāfa|

baby ▪ *[353, n]*

■ رضـــيع □ <m> ▪ |raḍiiʕ|

boy ▪ *[354, n]*

■ ولـد □ <m> ▪ |walad|

man ▪ *[355, n]*

■ راجِل □ <m> ▪ |rāgil| □ [ˈrɑːgil]

girl ▪ *[356, n]*

■ بنــت □ <f> ▪ |bent|

woman ▪ *[357, n]*

■ ســت □ <f> ▪ |sitt| □ [sitˑ]

husband ▪ *[358, n]*

■ جوز □ <m> ▪ |goz|

wife ▪ *[359, n]*

■ زَوْجَة □ <f> ▪ |zawga|

family ▪ *[360, n]*

■ عيلـــة □ <f> ▪ |ˈéla|

father ▪ *[361, n]*

■ أب ▪ |ˈab|

mother ▪ *[362, n]*

■ ماما □ <f> ▪ |mama|

daughter ▪ *[363, n]*

■ بـت □ <f> ▪ |bett|

neighbour ▪ *[370, n]*

■ جار □ <m> ▪ |gār|

enemy ▪ *[372, n]*

■ عدو □ <m> ▪ |ˈadu|

religion ▪ *[373, n]*

■ ديـن □ <m> ▪ |dīn|

priest ▪ *[374, n]*

■ قســـيس □ <m> ▪ |ˈasīs, ˈesīs|

god ▪ *[376, n]*

■ إلـه □ <m> ▪ |ˈílāh|

art ▪ *[377, n]*

■ فـن □ <m> ▪ |fann|

photograph ▪ *[379, n]*

■ صورة ▪ |ṣūra|

song ▪ *[382, n]*

■ اغنيـة □ <f> ▪ |oḡneya|

newspaper ▪ *[392, n]*

	▪ جرنان □ <m> ▪ |gornān|
school ▪ *[394, n]*	
	▪ مدرسة □ <f> ▪ |madrasa|
university ▪ *[395, n]*	
	▪ جامعة □ <f> ▪ |gamʻa|
teacher ▪ *[397, n]*	
	▪ مدرس □ <m> ▪ |mudares|
student ▪ *[398, n]*	
	▪ طالب □ <m> ▪ |ṭāleb|
money ▪ *[401, n]*	
	▪ فلـــوس □ <pl> ▪ |felous| □ /fluːs/
job ▪ *[407, n]*	
	▪ وظيفـــة □ <f> ▪ |waẓiifa|
worker ▪ *[409, n]*	
	▪ عامل ▪ |ʕaamel|
price ▪ *[411, n]*	
	▪ تمـن □ <m> ▪ |tamn, taman|
gift ▪ *[412, n]*	
	▪ هدية □ <f> ▪ |hedeya|
farmer ▪ *[416, n]*	
	▪ فــلاح □ <m> ▪ |fallaaḥ|
scissors ▪ *[418, n]*	
	▪ مَقَصّ □ <m> ▪ |maqaṣṣ|
key ▪ *[420, n]*	
	▪ مفتــاح ▪ |muftāḥ|
lawyer ▪ *[430, n]*	
	▪ محامي □ <m> ▪ |muḥāmī|
king ▪ *[434, n]*	
	▪ ملك □ <m> ▪ |malek|
stadium ▪ *[444, n]*	
	▪ اســتاد □ <m> ▪ |estād|
dance ▪ *[445, n]*	
	▪ رقص □ <m> ▪ |raʔṣ|
game ▪ *[446, n]*	
	▪ لعـب □ <m> ▪ |leʻb|
toy ▪ *[448, n]*	
	▪ عروسة □ <f> ▪ |ʕaruusa|
not ▪ *[450, sv]*	
	▪ مش ▪ |miš / muš|
can ▪ *[451, sv]*	
	▪ قـدر ▪ |'adar|
must ▪ *[453, sv]*	

88

■ لازم □ {adjective} ■ |lāzim|

live ▪ *[456, v]*

■ عَاش ■ |ʿāš|

die ▪ *[457, v]*

■ مات ■ |maat|

open ▪ *[471, v]*

■ فتـــح ■ |fataḥ|

be ▪ *[478, v]* ▪ *to occupy place*

■ كان ■ |kan|

go ▪ *[483, v]*

■ راح ■ |rāḥ|

return ▪ *[485, v]*

■ رجع ■ |regeʕ|

leave ▪ *[486, v]* ▪ *to depart*

■ مشـى ■ |mashaa|

come ▪ *[489, v]*

■ جا ■ |gā|

follow ▪ *[490, v]*

■ ورا يمشـــي ■ |yemši wara|

run ▪ *[492, v]*

■ جرى ■ |garā|

swim ▪ *[493, v]*

■ عام ■ |ʿām|

fly ▪ *[494, v]*

■ طار ■ |ṭār|

jump ▪ *[497, v]*

■ نـط ■ |naṭṭ|

pull ▪ *[498, v]*

■ شـد ■ |shadd|

push ▪ *[499, v]*

■ زق ■ |zaqq|

stand ▪ *[501, v]*

■ وقـف ■ |weʔef|

take ▪ *[509, v]*

■ خد ■ |xad|

give ▪ *[512, v]*

■ ادى ■ |eda|

carry ▪ *[514, v]*

■ شـال ■ |šaal|

bring ▪ *[515, v]*

■ جاب ■ |gāb|

send ▪ *[516, v]*

■ بعـت ■ |baʿat|

prepare ▪ [524, v]

■ جهز ■ |gahezz|

save ▪ [533, v] ▪ to help to survive

■ أنقـذ ■ |ʾanqaz|

wait ▪ [539, v]

■ اسـتنى ■ |istanna|

drive ▪ [541, v]

■ سـاق ■ |sāʾ|

wear ▪ [543, v]

■ لبـس ■ |libis|

cough ▪ [545, v]

■ كح ■ |kaḥ|

kiss ▪ [546, v]

■ بَاس ■ |bās|

drink ▪ [552, v]

■ شـرب ■ |širib|

look ▪ [558, v]

■ بـص ■ |baṣṣ| □ /bɑsˤː/

see ▪ [559, v]

■ شـاف ■ |šāf|

listen ▪ [560, v]

■ سـمع ■ |simiʿ|

hear ▪ [561, v]

■ سـمع ■ |simiʿ|

taste ▪ [562, v]

■ داق ■ |daaq|

hide ▪ [567, v]

■ خفـى ■ |ḵafa|

forget ▪ [572, v]

■ نسـي ■ |nisii|

understand ▪ [573, v]

■ فهـم ■ |fihim|

think ▪ [574, v]

■ فَكَّرَ ■ |fakkara|

know ▪ [575, v] ▪ to be sure about

■ عرف ■ |ʿeref|

miss ▪ [596, v]

■ وحش ■ |waHish|

love ▪ [597, v]

■ حب ■ |ḥab| □ /ħæbː/

want ▪ [598, v]

■ عـايز ■ |ʿāyiz|

■ عاوز □ {adjective} ■ |ʿāwiz|

hope ▪ [599, v]

■ اتمـنى ■ |atmanā|

hate ▪ [600, v]

■ كـره ■ |kirih|

say ▪ [608, v]

■ قـال ■ |ʾāl|

tell ▪ [611, v]

■ قـال ■ |ʔaal|

escape ▪ [632, v]

■ زوغ ■ |zawwaḡ|

sing ▪ [637, v]

■ غـنى ■ |ḡanā|

sell ▪ [640, v]

■ بـاع ■ |bāʿ|

buy ▪ [641, v]

■ اشـترى ■ |ištarā|

kill ▪ [646, v]

■ قتـل ■ |ʔatal|

alive ▪ [650, adj]

■ عـايش ■ |ʕaayesh|

empty ▪ [660, adj]

■ فاضـي ■ |faḍi|

full ▪ [661, adj] ▪ containing maximum

■ مليـان ■ |malyaan|

small ▪ [662, adj]

■ صـغير ■ |ṣuḡayyar|

big ▪ [663, adj]

■ كبـير ■ |kibīr|

short ▪ [665, adj] ▪ of size

■ قصـير ■ |ʾuṣáyyar|

long ▪ [666, adj] ▪ of size

■ طويـل ■ |ṭawīl|

low ▪ [667, adj]

■ واطي ■ |waṭi|

high ▪ [668, adj]

■ عـالي ■ |ʕaali|

narrow ▪ [669, adj]

■ ضـيق ■ |dayaʾ|

wide ▪ [670, adj]

■ واسـع ■ |wāseʿ|

thin ▪ [671, adj]

▪ رفيــع <f> ▪ □ | rofayyaʔ |

heavy ▪ [674, adj]

▪ تقيـــل ▪ | tiʼīl |

bright ▪ [676, adj]

▪ منور ▪ | menawar |

red ▪ [683, adj]

▪ أحمر ▪ | ʼaḥmar |

flat ▪ [696, adj]

▪ مسـطح ▪ | meṣaṭṭaḥ |

far ▪ [703, adj]

▪ بعيــد ▪ | beʼīd |

new ▪ [715, adj]

▪ جديـد ▪ | gdiid |

young ▪ [716, adj]

▪ شـب ▪ | šab |

old ▪ [717, adj]

▪ عجوز ▪ | ʼagoz |

dangerous ▪ [723, adj]

▪ خطيـر ▪ | xaṭir |

previous ▪ [730, adj]

▪ قبـل ▪ | ʔabl |

next ▪ [731, adj]

▪ جي الـي ▪ | eli gai |

female ▪ [733, adj]

▪ أنـثى <f> ▪ □ | onθa or onsa |

ill ▪ [737, adj]

▪ عيـان ▪ | ʼayyān |

bad ▪ [753, adj] ▪ of evaluation

▪ وحش ▪ | wiḥš |

main ▪ [758, adj]

▪ رئيسـي ▪ | raʔiisi |

correct ▪ [766, adj]

▪ صَح ▪ | ṣaḥ |

cheap ▪ [795, adj]

▪ رخيـص ▪ | rikīṣ |

why ▪ [797, adv]

▪ ليـه ▪ | lēh | □ /le:/

how ▪ [799, adv] ▪ in what state

▪ ازاي ▪ | izzayy |

how ▪ [800, adv] ▪ to what degree

▪ إزي ▪ | izzayy |

very ▪ *[803, adv]*

▪ جدا ▪ |gedan|

also ▪ *[808, adv]*

▪ كمان ▪ |kaman, kman|

up ▪ *[812, adv]*

▪ فــوق ▪ |fooʾ|

away ▪ *[818, adv]*

▪ بعيـــد ▪ |beʾīd|

here ▪ *[823, adv]*

▪ هنا ▪ |hena|

there ▪ *[824, adv]* ▪ *place*

▪ هناك ▪ |hinaak|

when ▪ *[825, adv]*

▪ امـتى ▪ |imta| ▫ [ˈemtæ]

ago ▪ *[827, adv]*

▪ من ▪ |men|

yesterday ▪ *[828, adv]*

▪ امبـارح ▪ |imbāraḥ|

today ▪ *[830, adv]*

▪ النهـارده ▪ |el-nahār-da| ▫ /ɪnːeˈharˤda/

now ▪ *[831, adv]*

▪ دلوقــتي ▪ |dilwaʾti|

tomorrow ▪ *[832, adv]*

▪ بكــرة South ▪ |bukra|

always ▪ *[833, adv]*

▪ ديمـا ▪ |dayman|

again ▪ *[837, adv]*

▪ تــاني ▪ |tani| ▫ /taːni/

early ▪ *[842, adv]*

▪ بــدري ▪ |badri|

already ▪ *[845, adv]*

▪ خلاص ▪ |ḥalaṣ|

maybe ▪ *[848, adv]*

▪ يمكــن ▪ |yimkin|

how ▪ *[849, adv]* ▪ *in what manner*

▪ إزي ▪ |izzayy|

I ▪ *[850, prn]*

▪ انـا ▪ |ana|

we ▪ *[851, prn]*

▪ احنـا ▪ |ˈíḥna|

you ▪ *[852, prn]* ▪ *subject <sg>*

▪ انـت <m> ▫ ▪ |ínta|

■ انــتي □ <f> ■ |ínti|

■ انتــوا □ <pl> ■ |intu|

you ▪ *[853, prn]* ▪ *subject <pl>*

■ إنتــوا □ <pl> ■ |íntu|

he ▪ *[854, prn]*

هو ■ |hówwa|

she ▪ *[855, prn]*

هي ■ |heyya|

they ▪ *[857, prn]*

هما ■ |humma|

me ▪ *[858, prn]*

ــني ■ |-ni|

us ▪ *[859, prn]*

ــنا ■ |-naa|

you ▪ *[860, prn]* ▪ *object <sg>*

■ ــك ■

you ▪ *[861, prn]* ▪ *object <pl>*

■ ــكو ■

her ▪ *[863, prn]*

ــها ■ |-ha|

them ▪ *[865, prn]*

ــهم ■ |-hum|

everything ▪ *[867, prn]*

حاجة كل ■ |kul ḥaga|

something ▪ *[869, prn]*

حاجة □ <f> ■ |ḥāga|

no one ▪ *[870, prn]*

ماحدش ■ |maḥaddiš|

nothing ▪ *[871, prn]*

حاجة ولا ■ |wala ḥaga|

what ▪ *[873, prn]*

ايـه ■ |ēh| □ [ʔeː(h)]

who ▪ *[874, prn]*

مين ■ |mīn| □ /miːn/

that ▪ *[876, det]*

دا هناك إلـي ■ |ili hnak da|

this ▪ *[877, det]*

ده □ <m> ■ |da|

no ▪ *[878, det]*

لاء ■ |la'|

both ▪ *[880, det]*

الاتنيــن ■ |letnīn|

94

same ▪ *[881, det]*

▪ نفســـه ▪ |náfsu|

my ▪ *[884, det]*

▪ ـي ▪ |-i|

our ▪ *[885, det]*

▪ ـنا ▪ |naa|

your ▪ *[886, det]* ▪ *<sg>*

▪ ك ▫ {owner is male} ▪ |-ak, k|

▪ ك ▫ {owner is female} ▪ |-ek, ki|

▪ بتاعــك ▪ |bita3ak|

your ▪ *[887, det]* ▪ *<pl>*

▪ ـكو ▪ |ku|

his ▪ *[888, det]*

▪ ـه ▪ |-u|

▪ بتـــاعو ليـه ▫ {possessive pronoun} ▪ |li betaʕo|

her ▪ *[889, det]*

▪ ـها ▪ |-ha|

their ▪ *[891, det]*

▪ ـهم ▪ |-hum|

few ▪ *[893, det]*

▪ شــوية ▪ |šuwayya|

many ▪ *[894, det]*

▪ كتـــير ▪ |kitīr|

more ▪ *[895, det]*

▪ أكـتر ▪ |ʔaktar|

enough ▪ *[897, det]*

▪ كفايـــة ▪ |kefaya|

one ▪ *[900, num]*

▪ واحد ▫ <m> ▪ |waḥed|

two ▪ *[901, num]*

▪ اتنيــن ▪ |itnēn| ▫ [ɪtˈneːn]

three ▪ *[902, num]*

▪ تلاتـــة ▪ |talāta| ▫ [tæˈlɛːtæ]

five ▪ *[904, num]*

▪ خمسة ▪ |ḵamsa| ▫ [ˈχɑmsɑ]

seven ▪ *[906, num]*

▪ ســبعة ▪ |sabaʿa| ▫ [ˈsæbʕæ]

eight ▪ *[907, num]*

▪ تمانيـــة ▪ |tamāniyya| ▫ [tæˈmænjæ]

nine ▪ *[908, num]*

▪ تســـعة ▪ |tisʿa| ▫ [ˈtɪsʕæ]

ten ▪ *[909, num]*

▪ عَشْرَة ▪ |ʿašra| ▫ [ˈʕaʃarˤa]

eleven ▪ [910, num]

▪ حداشر ▪ |ḥidaašar| ▫ [ħɪˈdaːʃarˤ]

twelve ▪ [911, num]

▪ اتناشـــر ▪ |itnašar| ▫ /ɪtˈnaːʃarˤ/

thirteen ▪ [912, num]

▪ تلاتاشـــر ▪ |talataašar| ▫ [talaˈtːaːʃarˤ]

fifteen ▪ [913, num]

▪ خمستاشـــر ▪ |ḵamastāšar| ▫ [χamasˈtaːʃarˤ]

twenty ▪ [914, num]

▪ عشـــرين ▪ |ʿešrīn|

thirty ▪ [915, num]

▪ تلاتيـــن ▪ |talātīn| ▫ /talatiːn/

fifty ▪ [916, num]

▪ خمسـين ▪ |xamsīn|

hundred ▪ [917, num]

▪ مية ▪ |miyya| ▫ /ˈmɪjːæ/

first ▪ [920, num]

▪ أول ▪ |ʾawwil|

second ▪ [921, num]

▪ تـــاني ▪ |tāniyy|

third ▪ [922, num]

▪ تالـــت ▪ |tālit| ▫ /taːlit/

and ▪ [925, cnj] ▪ similar words

▪ و ▪ |we|

but ▪ [928, cnj]

▪ بـس ▪ |bas|

that ▪ [930, cnj]

▪ ان ▪ |ʾinn|

while ▪ [933, cnj]

▪ لمـا ▪ |lama|

where ▪ [934, cnj]

▪ فيـــن ▪ |feen|

because ▪ [935, cnj]

▪ علشـــان ▪ |ʿalašān|

if ▪ [937, cnj] ▪ supposing that

▪ اذا ▪ |eza|

if ▪ [939, cnj] ▪ whether

▪ إذا ▪ |ʾeza|

as ▪ [940, cnj]

▪ زي ▪ |zai|

by ▪ [944, prp]

■ ـبـ ■ | be |

for ▪ *[946, prp]* ▪ *because of*

■ عشـان ■ | ʿašaan |

for ▪ *[947, prp]* ▪ *intended to*

■ ـلـ ■ | le |

about ▪ *[948, prp]* ▪ *concerning*

■ عن ■ | ʿan |

than ▪ *[949, prp]*

■ من ■ | men |

like ▪ *[950, prp]*

■ زي ■ | zayy |

without ▪ *[952, prp]*

■ غـير من ■ | men ġer |

from ▪ *[953, prp]* ▪ *with source*

■ من ■ | men |

from ▪ *[954, prp]* ▪ *with starting point*

■ من ■ | men |

to ▪ *[955, prp]* ▪ *direction*

■ ـلـ ■ | le |

into ▪ *[956, prp]*

■ جوا ■ | gowa |

against ▪ *[958, prp]* ▪ *direction*

■ ضـد ■ | ḍedd |

along ▪ *[959, prp]*

■ طول عـلـى ■ | ʿalaa ṭuul |

at ▪ *[963, prp]* ▪ *place*

■ عنـد ■ | ʿand |

outside ▪ *[965, prp]*

■ بـرا ■ | baraa |

on ▪ *[966, prp]* ▪ *place*

■ عـلـى ■ | ʿala |

above ▪ *[967, prp]*

■ فـوق ■ | fawq | ▫ /foːʔ/

under ▪ *[968, prp]*

■ تحـت ■ | taḥt |

behind ▪ *[970, prp]* ▪ *place*

■ ورا ■ | warā |

between ▪ *[971, prp]*

■ بيـن ■ | ben |

about ▪ *[972, prp]* ▪ *on every side*

■ حـولين ■ | ḥawalén |

near ▪ *[974, prp]*

• جنــب • |ganb|

at • [975, prp] • time

• فــي • |fi|

during • [977, prp]

• خلال • |ķelaal|

until • [980, prp]

• حــتى • |leghayyet|

before • [981, prp] • earlier than

• قبــل • |'abl|

after • [982, prp] • later than

• بعــد • |ba3d| ▫ [bæːht]

hi • [984, int]

• أَهْلًا • |'ahlan|

yes • [996, int]

• أَيْوَة • |áywa|

no • [997, int]

• لَا • |la'|

[MLT] MALTESE. SURVIVAL DICTIONARY

thing ▪ [001, n]
　　　　　　▪ ħaġa ▫ <f> ▪ /ˈħaːdʒe/
part ▪ [003, n]
　　　　　　▪ parti ▪
half ▪ [004, n]
　　　　　　▪ nofs ▫ <m> ▪ /nɔfs/
cross ▪ [009, n]
　　　　　　▪ salib ▫ <m> ▪ /seˈliːp/
circle ▪ [020, n]
　　　　　　▪ ċirku ▪ /ˈtʃɪrkʊ/
rope ▪ [026, n]
　　　　　　▪ ħabel ▫ <m> ▪
ruler ▪ [031, n]
　　　　　　▪ riga ▫ <f> ▪
kilogram ▪ [034, n]
　　　　　　▪ kilogramm ▫ <m> ▪
light ▪ [035, n]
　　　　　　▪ dawl ▫ <m> ▪ /dawl/
color ▪ [036, n]
　　　　　　▪ kulur ▫ <m> ▪
sound ▪ [037, n]
　　　　　　▪ ħoss ▫ <m> ▪
temperature ▪ [039, n]
　　　　　　▪ temperatura ▫ <f> ▪
smell ▪ [042, n]
　　　　　　▪ riħa ▫ <f> ▪
gas ▪ [043, n]
　　　　　　▪ gass ▫ <m> ▪
fire ▪ [046, n]
　　　　　　▪ nar ▫ <f> ▪
smoke ▪ [047, n]
　　　　　　▪ duħħan ▪
gold ▪ [050, n]
　　　　　　▪ deheb ▫ <m/f> ▪ /ˈdɛːp/
iron ▪ [051, n]
　　　　　　▪ ħadid ▫ <m> ▪ /ħeˈdiːt/
silver ▪ [052, n]
　　　　　　▪ fidda ▫ <f> ▪ /ˈfɪdːe/
water ▪ [053, n]
　　　　　　▪ ilma ▪ /ˈɪlme/

ice ▪ *[054, n]*

    ▪ silġ ▫ \<m> ▪ /sɪltʃ/

air ▪ *[055, n]*

    ▪ arja ▫ \<f> ▪

sand ▪ *[056, n]*

    ▪ ramel ▫ \<m> ▪

glass ▪ *[059, n]* ▪ *substance*

    ▪ ħġieġ ▫ \<m> ▪ /ħdʒɪːtʃ/

paint ▪ *[060, n]*

    ▪ żebgħa ▫ \<f> ▪

paper ▪ *[062, n]*

    ▪ karta ▫ \<f> ▪

leather ▪ *[064, n]*

    ▪ ġilda ▫ \<f> ▪ /ˈdʒɪldə/

gasoline ▪ *[065, n]*

    ▪ petrol ▫ \<m> ▪

soap ▪ *[067, n]*

    ▪ sapuna ▫ \<f> ▪

east ▪ *[071, n]*

    ▪ lvant ▪

north ▪ *[072, n]*

    ▪ tramuntana ▪

south ▪ *[073, n]*

    ▪ nofsinhar ▪

west ▪ *[074, n]*

    ▪ punent ▪

place ▪ *[075, n]*

    ▪ lok ▫ \<m> ▪

time ▪ *[076, n]* ▪ *passing of events*

    ▪ darba ▫ \<f> ▪

hour ▪ *[077, n]*

    ▪ siegħa ▪

minute ▪ *[078, n]*

    ▪ minuta ▫ \<f> ▪

second ▪ *[079, n]*

    ▪ sekonda ▫ \<f> ▪ /sɛˈkɔndə/

afternoon ▪ *[081, n]*

    ▪ waranofsinhar ▫ \<m> ▪

evening ▪ *[082, n]*

    ▪ għaxija ▫ \<f> ▪

night ▪ *[084, n]*

    ▪ lejl ▫ \<m> ▪ /lɛjl/

week ▪ *[085, n]*
  ▪ ġimgħa ▪
year ▪ *[086, n]*
  ▪ sena ▫ <f> ▪ /ˈsɛne/
month ▪ *[087, n]*
  ▪ xahar ▪ /ʃar/
autumn ▪ *[089, n]*
  ▪ ħarifa ▫ <f> ▪ /ħeˈriːfe/
spring ▪ *[090, n]*
  ▪ rebbiegħa ▫ <f> ▪ /rɛˈbːɪˤːe/
summer ▪ *[091, n]*
  ▪ sajf ▫ <m> ▪ /seɪ̯f/
winter ▪ *[092, n]*
  ▪ xitwa ▪ /ˈʃɪtwe/
century ▪ *[093, n]*
  ▪ seklu ▪
history ▪ *[095, n]*
  ▪ storja ▫ <f> ▪
holiday ▪ *[097, n]*
  ▪ jum il-festa ▪
birthday ▪ *[098, n]*
  ▪ għeluq snin ▪
wedding ▪ *[099, n]*
  ▪ tieġ ▫ <m> ▪ /tɪːtʃ/
end ▪ *[103, n]*
  ▪ tmiem ▪ /tmɪːm/
clock ▪ *[104, n]*
  ▪ arloġġ ▫ <m> ▪ /erˈlɔtɕː/
star ▪ *[106, n]*
  ▪ niġma ▫ <f> ▪
moon ▪ *[107, n]*
  ▪ qamar ▫ <m> ▪ [ˈʔaːmer]
sun ▪ *[108, n]*
  ▪ xemx ▫ <m> ▪ /ʃɛmʃ/
sky ▪ *[109, n]*
  ▪ sema ▫ <m> ▪
weather ▪ *[110, n]*
  ▪ temp ▫ <m> ▪
cloud ▪ *[111, n]*
  ▪ sħaba ▫ <f> ▪ /ˈsħaːbe/
fog ▪ *[112, n]*
  ▪ ċpar ▫ <m> ▪

rain ▪ *[113, n]*

　　　　▪ xita ▫ <f> ▪ /'ʃɪte/

snow ▪ *[114, n]*

　　　　▪ borra ▫ <m> ▪

wind ▪ *[115, n]*

　　　　▪ riħ ▫ <f> ▪ /riːħ/

sea ▪ *[116, n]*

　　　　▪ baħar ▫ <m> ▪ /'baːħer/

lake ▪ *[117, n]*

　　　　▪ għadira ▫ <f> ▪ /aˤːˈdiːr/

river ▪ *[118, n]*

　　　　▪ xmara ▫ <f> ▪ /'ʃmeːre/

wave ▪ *[119, n]*

　　　　▪ mewġa ▫ <f> ▪

mountain ▪ *[122, n]*

　　　　▪ muntanja ▫ <f> ▪

cave ▪ *[123, n]*

　　　　▪ għar ▫ <m> ▪ /aːr/

country ▪ *[125, n]*

　　　　▪ pajjiż ▫ <m> ▪ /pejːɪs/

border ▪ *[126, n]*

　　　　▪ fruntiera ▫ <f> ▪

island ▪ *[127, n]*

　　　　▪ gżira ▫ <f> ▪ /'gziːre/

desert ▪ *[128, n]*

　　　　▪ deżert ▫ <m> ▪

forest ▪ *[129, n]*

　　　　▪ foresta ▫ <f> ▪

city ▪ *[130, n]*

　　　　▪ belt ▪ /'bɛlt/

town ▪ *[131, n]*

　　　　▪ raħal ▪ /'reħel/

village ▪ *[132, n]*

　　　　▪ villaġġ ▫ <m> ▪

park ▪ *[133, n]*

　　　　▪ park ▫ <m> ▪

road ▪ *[134, n]*

　　　　▪ triq ▫ <f> ▪ /triːʔ/

street ▪ *[135, n]*

　　　　▪ triq ▫ <f> ▪ /triːʔ/

bridge ▪ *[137, n]*

　　　　▪ pont ▫ <m> ▪

building ▪ *[139, n]*
> ▪ binja ▫ <f> ▪

house ▪ *[140, n]*
> ▪ bejt ▫ <m> ▪ /bɛɪ̯t/

station ▪ *[141, n]*
> ▪ istazzjon ▪

airport ▪ *[142, n]*
> ▪ ajruport ▪

port ▪ *[143, n]*
> ▪ port ▫ <m> ▪

roof ▪ *[144, n]*
> ▪ saqaf ▫ <m> ▪ /ˈseʔef/

floor ▪ *[146, n]*
> ▪ art ▫ <f> ▪

ceiling ▪ *[147, n]*
> ▪ saqaf ▫ <m> ▪ /ˈseʔef/

door ▪ *[148, n]*
> ▪ bieb ▫ <m> ▪ /ˈbɪːp/

window ▪ *[149, n]*
> ▪ tieqa ▫ <f> ▪

stairs ▪ *[150, n]*
> ▪ tat-turġien ▪

room ▪ *[151, n]*
> ▪ kamra ▫ <f> ▪

bathroom ▪ *[152, n]*
> ▪ kamra tal-banju ▪

home ▪ *[155, n]*
> ▪ dar ▪

hotel ▪ *[156, n]*
> ▪ lukanda ▫ <m> ▪ /lʊˈkendɐ/

chair ▪ *[157, n]*
> ▪ siġġu ▫ <m> ▪ /ˈsɪdːʒʊ/

bed ▪ *[158, n]*
> ▪ sodda ▪ /ˈsɔdːɐ/

table ▪ *[160, n]*
> ▪ mejda ▫ <f> ▪

shelf ▪ *[161, n]*
> ▪ xkaffa ▫ <f> ▪

mirror ▪ *[162, n]*
> ▪ mera ▫ <f> ▪ /ˈmɛːrɐ/

carpet ▪ *[163, n]*
> ▪ tapit ▫ <m> ▪

blanket ▪ *[164, n]*
        ▪ kutra ▫ <f> ▪ /ˈkuːt.ra/

pillow ▪ *[165, n]*
        ▪ mħadda ▫ <f> ▪ /ˈmħedːe/

towel ▪ *[166, n]*
        ▪ xugaman ▫ <m> ▪

curtain ▪ *[167, n]*
        ▪ purtiera ▫ <f> ▪

cup ▪ *[169, n]*
        ▪ kikkra ▫ <f> ▪

glass ▪ *[170, n]* ▪ *vessel*
        ▪ tazza ▫ <f> ▪

plate ▪ *[171, n]*
        ▪ pjanċa ▫ <f> ▪

fork ▪ *[172, n]*
        ▪ furketta ▫ <f> ▪ /fʊrˈkɛt.ta/

knife ▪ *[173, n]*
        ▪ sikkina ▫ <f> ▪ /sɪˈkiːne/

spoon ▪ *[174, n]*
        ▪ mgħarfa ▫ <f> ▪

bottle ▪ *[176, n]*
        ▪ flixkun ▪

machine ▪ *[179, n]*
        ▪ magna ▫ <f> ▪

engine ▪ *[181, n]*
        ▪ mutur ▫ <m> ▪

refrigerator ▪ *[183, n]*
        ▪ friġġ ▫ <m> ▪

lamp ▪ *[185, n]*
        ▪ lampa ▫ <f> ▪

shower ▪ *[187, n]*
        ▪ doċċa ▫ <f> ▪

toilet ▪ *[188, n]*
        ▪ tojlit ▫ <m> ▪

television ▪ *[189, n]* ▪ *device*
        ▪ televiżjoni ▫ <f> ▪

telephone ▪ *[191, n]*
        ▪ telefon ▫ <m> ▪

computer ▪ *[192, n]*
        ▪ kompjuter ▫ <m> ▪

file ▪ *[193, n]*
        ▪ fajl ▫ <m> ▪

bus ▪ *[195, n]*
- xarabank ▫ <m> ▪

car ▪ *[196, n]*
- karozza ▫ <f> ▪

truck ▪ *[197, n]*
- trakk ▪

bicycle ▪ *[198, n]*
- rota ▪

boat ▪ *[200, n]*
- dgħajsa ▫ <f> ▪ /ˈdaˤːjsɐ/

ship ▪ *[201, n]*
- vapur ▫ <m> ▪

airplane ▪ *[202, n]*
- ajruplan ▫ <m> ▪

driver ▪ *[203, n]*
- sewwieq ▫ <m> ▪

ticket ▪ *[205, n]*
- biljett ▫ <m> ▪

dress ▪ *[207, n]*
- libsa ▫ <f> ▪

jacket ▪ *[209, n]*
- ġaketta ▫ <f> ▪

shirt ▪ *[210, n]*
- qmis ▫ <f> ▪ /ʔmiːs/

pants ▪ *[212, n]*
- qalziet ▫ <m> ▪ /ʔalˈt͡sɪːt/

skirt ▪ *[213, n]*
- dublett ▫ <m> ▪

hat ▪ *[215, n]*
- hat ▪

boot ▪ *[216, n]*
- buzza ▫ <f> ▪

shoe ▪ *[217, n]*
- żarbuna ▫ <f> ▪

scarf ▪ *[218, n]*
- xalla ▫ <f> ▪

umbrella ▪ *[219, n]*
- umbrella ▫ <f> ▪ /ʊmbˈrɛlːɐ/

ring ▪ *[220, n]*
- ċurkett ▫ <m> ▪

mushroom ▪ *[222, n]*
- faqqiegħa ▫ <m> ▪

grass ▪ *[223, n]*

▪ ħaxix ▫ <m> ▪ /ħeˈʃiːʃ/

tree ▪ *[224, n]*

▪ siġra ▫ <f> ▪ /ˈsɪdʒre/

leaf ▪ *[225, n]*

▪ werqa ▫ <f> ▪ /ˈwɛrʔe/

flower ▪ *[226, n]*

▪ fjura ▫ <f> ▪ /ˈfjuːre/

animal ▪ *[227, n]*

▪ annimal ▫ <m> ▪

cat ▪ *[228, n]*

▪ qattus ▫ <m> ▪ /ʔeˈtːuːs/

dog ▪ *[229, n]*

▪ kelb ▫ <m> ▪ /kɛlp/

horse ▪ *[230, n]*

▪ żiemel ▫ <m> ▪ /ˈzɪːmɛl/

sheep ▪ *[231, n]*

▪ nagħġa ▫ <f> ▪

pig ▪ *[232, n]*

▪ ħanżir ▫ <m> ▪ /ħenˈziːr/

cow ▪ *[233, n]*

▪ baqra ▫ <f> ▪ /ˈbeʔre/

lion ▪ *[234, n]*

▪ iljun ▫ <m> ▪

bear ▪ *[235, n]*

▪ ors ▫ <m> ▪

elephant ▪ *[236, n]*

▪ iljunfant ▪

mouse ▪ *[237, n]*

▪ ġurdien ▫ <m> ▪ /dʐʊrˈdɪːn/

monkey ▪ *[238, n]*

▪ xadin ▫ <m> ▪ /ʃeˈdɪːn/

snake ▪ *[239, n]*

▪ serp ▫ <m> ▪

frog ▪ *[240, n]*

▪ żrinġ ▫ <m> ▪ /zrɪntʃ/

bird ▪ *[241, n]*

▪ għasfur ▫ <m> ▪ /asˈfuːr/

chicken ▪ *[242, n]*

▪ fellus ▫ <m> ▪ /fɛˈlːuːs/

duck ▪ *[243, n]*

▪ papra ▫ <f> ▪ /ˈpepre/

fish ▪ *[244, n]*
- ħuta ▫ <f> ▪

insect ▪ *[245, n]*
- insett ▫ <m> ▪ /ɪnˈsɛtː/

fly ▪ *[246, n]*
- dubbiena ▫ <f> ▪ /dʊˈbɪːne/

body ▪ *[247, n]*
- ġisem ▫ <m> ▪ /ˈdʒiːsɛm/

back ▪ *[248, n]* ▪ *of body*
- dahar ▫ <m> ▪

belly ▪ *[249, n]*
- żaqq ▫ <m> ▪ /zeʔ/

head ▪ *[251, n]*
- ras ▪ /ˈreːs/

leg ▪ *[254, n]*
- riġel ▪ /ˈrɪd͡ʒɛl/

arm ▪ *[255, n]*
- driegħ ▫ <m> ▪ /drɪːħ/

finger ▪ *[256, n]*
- saba ▫ <m> ▪

hand ▪ *[257, n]*
- id ▫ <f> ▪

blood ▪ *[258, n]*
- demm ▫ <m> ▪ /dɛmː/

heart ▪ *[259, n]*
- qalb ▫ <m> ▪ /ˈʔelp/

brain ▪ *[260, n]*
- moħħ ▫ <m> ▪ /ˈmɔħː/

stomach ▪ *[261, n]*
- stonku ▫ <m> ▪ /ˈstɔnkʊ/

bone ▪ *[263, n]*
- għadma ▫ <f> ▪ /ˈaˤːdme/

health ▪ *[265, n]*
- saħħa ▫ <f> ▪

disease ▪ *[266, n]*
- marda ▫ <f> ▪

pain ▪ *[267, n]*
- uġigħ ▫ <m> ▪ /ʊˈdʒiːħ/

spectacles ▪ *[270, n]*
- nuċċalijiet ▫ <pl> ▪

hospital ▪ *[271, n]*
- sptar ▪

doctor ▪ *[272, n]*
        ▪ tabib ▫ <m> ▪ /tɛˈbip/

cigarette ▪ *[273, n]*
        ▪ sigaretti ▪

face ▪ *[274, n]*
        ▪ wiċċ ▫ <m> ▪ /wɪt͡ʃː/

eye ▪ *[275, n]*
        ▪ għajn ▫ <f> ▪ /aˤːjn/

ear ▪ *[276, n]*
        ▪ widna ▫ <f> ▪ /ˈwɪdnɐ/

nose ▪ *[277, n]*
        ▪ mnieħer ▫ <m> ▪

mouth ▪ *[278, n]*
        ▪ ħalq ▫ <m> ▪ /ħelʔ/

hair ▪ *[279, n]*
        ▪ xagħar ▫ <m> ▪ /ʃaˤːr/

food ▪ *[280, n]*
        ▪ ikel ▫ <m> ▪ /ˈɪkɛl/

breakfast ▪ *[281, n]*
        ▪ kolazzjon ▫ <m> ▪

lunch ▪ *[282, n]*
        ▪ ikla ▫ <f> ▪

dinner ▪ *[283, n]*
        ▪ ċena ▫ <f> ▪

cook ▪ *[284, n]*
        ▪ kok ▫ <m> ▪

soup ▪ *[287, n]*
        ▪ soppa ▫ <f> ▪

onion ▪ *[288, n]*
        ▪ basla ▫ <f> ▪

tomato ▪ *[289, n]*
        ▪ tadam ▫ <m> ▪

potato ▪ *[290, n]*
        ▪ patata ▫ <f> ▪ /pɛˈtaːtɐ/

apple ▪ *[291, n]*
        ▪ tuffieħa ▫ <f> ▪ /tʊˈfɪːħɐ/

orange ▪ *[292, n]*
        ▪ larinġa ▫ <f> ▪ /lɛˈrɪndʒɐ/

grape ▪ *[293, n]*
        ▪ għenba ▫ <f> ▪ /ˈɛˤːnbɐ/

nut ▪ *[294, n]*
        ▪ ġewża ▫ <f> ▪

rice • *[295, n]*
> • ross ◦ <m> •

bread • *[296, n]*
> • ħobż ◦ <m> • /ħɔps/

cheese • *[297, n]*
> • ġobon ◦ <m> • /ˈd͡ʒɔbɔn/

milk • *[298, n]*
> • ħalib ◦ <m> • /ħeˈliːp/

meat • *[300, n]*
> • laħam ◦ <m> •

sausage • *[301, n]*
> • salami ◦ <m> •

cake • *[302, n]*
> • kejk ◦ <m> •

chocolate • *[303, n]*
> • ċikkulata ◦ <f> •

sauce • *[305, n]*
> • zalza ◦ <f> •

spice • *[306, n]*
> • ħwawar •

salt • *[307, n]*
> • melħ ◦ <m> •

coffee • *[308, n]*
> • kafè ◦ <m> •

tea • *[309, n]*
> • te •

beer • *[310, n]*
> • birra ◦ <f> • /ˈbɪrːe/

wine • *[311, n]*
> • inbid ◦ <m> •

restaurant • *[312, n]*
> • restorant ◦ <m> •

dream • *[313, n]*
> • ħolma ◦ <f> • /ˈħɔlme/

information • *[315, n]*
> • informazzjoni ◦ <f> • /ɪnfɔrmeˈt͡sjɔːnɪ/

news • *[316, n]*
> • ġrajjiet kurenti ◦ <pl> •

memory • *[317, n]*
> • memorja ◦ <f> •

number • *[324, n]* • *of rank*
> • numru • /ˈnʊmrʊ/

letter ▪ *[327, n]* ▪ *message*
　　　　　　　▪ ittra ◦ <f> ▪ /ˈɪt.tra/
book ▪ *[328, n]*
　　　　　　　▪ ktieb ◦ <m> ▪
dictionary ▪ *[330, n]*
　　　　　　　▪ diz...narju ◦ <m> ▪ [dɪtːsjʊˈnerjʊ]
page ▪ *[331, n]*
　　　　　　　▪ paġna ▪
pen ▪ *[333, n]*
　　　　　　　▪ pinna ◦ <f> ▪
letter ▪ *[334, n]* ▪ *symbol*
　　　　　　　▪ ittra ◦ <f> ▪ /ˈɪt.tra/
flag ▪ *[336, n]*
　　　　　　　▪ bandiera ◦ <f> ▪ /benˈdɪːre/
name ▪ *[337, n]*
　　　　　　　▪ isem ◦ <m> ▪ /ˈiːsɛm/
word ▪ *[338, n]*
　　　　　　　▪ kelma ◦ <f> ▪ /ˈkɛlme/
language ▪ *[340, n]*
　　　　　　　▪ lingwa ▪ /ˈlɪngwe/
problem ▪ *[342, n]*
　　　　　　　▪ problema ◦ <f> ▪
mistake ▪ *[343, n]*
　　　　　　　▪ żball ◦ <m> ▪
habit ▪ *[344, n]*
　　　　　　　▪ drawwa ◦ <f> ▪
voice ▪ *[345, n]*
　　　　　　　▪ vuċi ◦ <f> ▪ /ˈvutʃɪ/
story ▪ *[347, n]*
　　　　　　　▪ storja ◦ <f> ▪
human ▪ *[348, n]*
　　　　　　　▪ bniedem ◦ <m> ◦ {male} ▪ /ˈbnɪːdɛm/
　　　　　　　▪ bniedma ◦ <f> ◦ {female} ▪
　　　　　　　▪ bnedmien pl ◦ {plural} ▪
culture ▪ *[349, n]*
　　　　　　　▪ kultura ▪
people ▪ *[351, n]*
　　　　　　　▪ nies ◦ <pl> ▪ [nɪːs]
baby ▪ *[353, n]*
　　　　　　　▪ tarbija ▪ /terˈbiːje/
boy ▪ *[354, n]*
　　　　　　　▪ tifel ◦ <m> ▪ /ˈtiːfɛl/

man ▪ *[355, n]*
　　　　　　　▪ raġel ▪ [ˈraːdʒɛl]
girl ▪ *[356, n]*
　　　　　　　▪ tfajla ▫ <f> ▪
woman ▪ *[357, n]*
　　　　　　　▪ mara ▪
husband ▪ *[358, n]*
　　　　　　　▪ raġel ▫ <m> ▪ [ˈraːdʒɛl]
wife ▪ *[359, n]*
　　　　　　　▪ mara ▫ <f> ▪
family ▪ *[360, n]*
　　　　　　　▪ familja ▫ <f> ▪
father ▪ *[361, n]*
　　　　　　　▪ missier ▪
daughter ▪ *[363, n]*
　　　　　　　▪ bint ▫ <f> ▪ /bɪnt/
son ▪ *[364, n]*
　　　　　　　▪ iben ▫ <m> ▪
sister ▪ *[366, n]*
　　　　　　　▪ oħt ▫ <f> ▪
friend ▪ *[369, n]*
　　　　　　　▪ ħabib ▫ <m> ▪ /ħeˈbiːp/
neighbour ▪ *[370, n]*
　　　　　　　▪ ġar ▫ <m> ▪ /d͡ʒaːr/
guest ▪ *[371, n]*
　　　　　　　▪ mistieden ▫ <m> ▪
enemy ▪ *[372, n]*
　　　　　　　▪ għadu ▫ <m> ▪
religion ▪ *[373, n]*
　　　　　　　▪ reliġjon ▪
priest ▪ *[374, n]*
　　　　　　　▪ qassis ▫ <m> ▪ /ʔeˈsːiːs/
temple ▪ *[375, n]*
　　　　　　　▪ tempju ▫ <m> ▪
god ▪ *[376, n]*
　　　　　　　▪ alla ▫ <m> ▪ /ˈelːe/
photograph ▪ *[379, n]*
　　　　　　　▪ ritratt ▫ <m> ▪
music ▪ *[381, n]*
　　　　　　　▪ mużika ▫ <f> ▪
song ▪ *[382, n]*
　　　　　　　▪ għanja ▫ <f> ▪ /aːnja/

guitar ▪ *[383, n]*
- kitarra ▫ <f> ▪

drum ▪ *[385, n]*
- tanbur ▫ <m> ▪

literature ▪ *[387, n]*
- letteratura ▫ <f> ▪

actor ▪ *[389, n]*
- attur ▫ <m> ▪

theater ▪ *[390, n]*
- teatru ▫ <m> ▪

television ▪ *[391, n]* ▪ *medium*
- televixin ▪ /tɛlɛvɪʒɪn/

newspaper ▪ *[392, n]*
- ġurnal ▫ <m> ▪

education ▪ *[393, n]*
- edukazzjoni ▪

school ▪ *[394, n]*
- skola ▪

university ▪ *[395, n]*
- università ▫ <f> ▪ /ʊnɪvɛrsɪˈta/

science ▪ *[396, n]*
- xjenza ▫ <f> ▪ /ˈʃjɛntsɛ/

teacher ▪ *[397, n]*
- għalliem ▫ <m> ▪

student ▪ *[398, n]*
- student ▫ <m> ▪

address ▪ *[399, n]*
- indirizz ▫ <m> ▪

money ▪ *[401, n]*
- flus ▫ <m pl> ▪

coin ▪ *[402, n]*
- munita ▫ <f> ▪

bank ▪ *[403, n]*
- bank ▫ <m> ▪

company ▪ *[406, n]*
- kumpanija ▫ <f> ▪

manager ▪ *[408, n]*
- meniġer ▫ <m> ▪

worker ▪ *[409, n]*
- ħaddiem ▫ <m> ▪

shop ▪ *[410, n]*
- ħanut ▫ <m> ▪

price ▪ *[411, n]*
> ▪ prezz ▫ <m> ▪

gift ▪ *[412, n]*
> ▪ rigal ▪

factory ▪ *[413, n]*
> ▪ fabbrika ▫ <f> ▪

engineer ▪ *[414, n]*
> ▪ inġinier ▫ <m> ▪

farm ▪ *[415, n]*
> ▪ razzett ▪

farmer ▪ *[416, n]*
> ▪ biedwi ▫ <m> ▪

scissors ▪ *[418, n]*
> ▪ mqassijiet ▫ <m pl> ▪ /m.ʔas.sɪ'jɪːt/

key ▪ *[420, n]*
> ▪ ċavetta ▫ <f> ▪ /tɕɑ'vɛttɑ/

document ▪ *[422, n]*
> ▪ dokument ▫ <m> ▪

passport ▪ *[423, n]*
> ▪ passaport ▫ <m> ▪

law ▪ *[425, n]*
> ▪ liġi ▪

police ▪ *[428, n]*
> ▪ pulizija ▫ <f> ▪

police officer ▪ *[429, n]*
> ▪ uffiċċjal tal-pulizija ▪

lawyer ▪ *[430, n]*
> ▪ avukat ▫ <m> ▪

prison ▪ *[431, n]*
> ▪ ħabs ▫ <m> ▪ /ħaps/

president ▪ *[433, n]*
> ▪ president ▫ <m> ▪

king ▪ *[434, n]*
> ▪ re ▫ <m> ▪

army ▪ *[435, n]*
> ▪ armata ▫ <f> ▪

soldier ▪ *[436, n]*
> ▪ suldat ▫ <m> ▪

castle ▪ *[437, n]*
> ▪ kastell ▫ <m> ▪

war ▪ *[438, n]*
> ▪ gwerra ▫ <f> ▪

sword ▪ [440, n]
- sejf ▫ <m> ▪ /sɛɪ̯f/

bomb ▪ [442, n]
- bomba ▫ <f> ▪

sport ▪ [443, n]
- sport ▫ <m> ▪

stadium ▪ [444, n]
- stadju ▫ <m> ▪

dance ▪ [445, n]
- żfin ▪

chess ▪ [447, n]
- ċess ▪

not ▪ [450, sv]
- mhux ▪

can ▪ [451, sv]
- sata ▪

live ▪ [456, v]
- għex ▪ /ɛˤːʃ/

die ▪ [457, v]
- miet ▪ /mɪːt/

do ▪ [460, v]
- għamel ▪ [aˤːmɛl]

become ▪ [464, v]
- sar ▪

break ▪ [466, v] ▪ to separate
- kiser ▪ /kɪsɛr/

open ▪ [471, v]
- fetaħ ▪ /ˈfɛːteħ/

boil ▪ [474, v]
- għalla ▪

go ▪ [483, v]
- mar ▪ /maːr/

come ▪ [489, v]
- ġie ▪

walk ▪ [491, v]
- mixi ▪

run ▪ [492, v]
- ġera ▪

jump ▪ [497, v]
- qabeż ▪ /ˈʔaːbɛs/

sit ▪ [502, v]
- qagħad ▪ /ʔaˤːt/

touch • *[505, v]*
• mess •

take • *[509, v]*
• ħa • /ħaː/

give • *[512, v]*
• ta •

bring • *[515, v]*
• ġab • /d͡ʒaːp/

have • *[517, v]*
• għand •

lose • *[519, v]* • ***to cease possesion***
• tilef •

need • *[523, v]*
• għand bżonn •

clean • *[529, v]*
• naddaf •

begin • *[535, v]*
• beda • /ˈbɛːdə/

wait • *[539, v]*
• stenna •

dress • *[542, v]*
• tlibes •

kiss • *[546, v]*
• bies • /bɪːs/

fuck • *[547, v]*
• niek • /nɪːk/

smoke • *[550, v]*
• pejjep •

drink • *[552, v]*
• xorob • [ˈʃɔrɔp]

sleep • *[555, v]*
• raqad • [ˈraːʔet]

dream • *[557, v]*
• ħolom •

see • *[559, v]*
• jara ▫ <imprf> •

listen • *[560, v]*
• issamma •

hear • *[561, v]*
• sama' • /ˈsɐmɐ/

forget • *[572, v]*
• nesa • /ˈnɛsɐ/

understand ▪ *[573, v]*
- fehem ▪ /fɛːm/

know ▪ *[575, v]* ▪ *to be sure about*
- għaf ▪

believe ▪ *[576, v]*
- emmen ▪

count ▪ *[580, v]*
- għadd ▪ /aːt/

read ▪ *[584, v]*
- qara ▪

write ▪ *[585, v]*
- kiteb ▪ [ˈkɪtɛp]

translate ▪ *[588, v]*
- ittraduċa ▪ /ɪtːreˈduːtʃe/

smile ▪ *[592, v]*
- tbissem ▪

cry ▪ *[593, v]*
- beka ▪

love ▪ *[597, v]*
- ħabb ▪ /ħɐpː/

want ▪ *[598, v]*
- ried ▪ /rɪːt/

hope ▪ *[599, v]*
- jittama ▪

hate ▪ *[600, v]*
- mibegħda ▪

choose ▪ *[602, v]*
- għażel ▪ /ˈaˁːzɛl/

speak ▪ *[607, v]*
- tkellem ▪

fight ▪ *[630, v]*
- ġlieda ▪

escape ▪ *[632, v]*
- ħarab ▪

win ▪ *[633, v]*
- rebaħ ▪ /ˈrɛːbeħ/

pray ▪ *[635, v]*
- talab ▪

sing ▪ *[637, v]*
- kanta ▪ /ˈkɐnte/

teach ▪ *[638, v]*
- għallem ▪

learn ▪ *[639, v]*
▪ tgħallem ▪

buy ▪ *[641, v]*
▪ xtara ▪ /ˈʃtaːre/

pay ▪ *[642, v]*
▪ ħallas ▪

hunt ▪ *[645, v]*
▪ kaċċa ▪

kill ▪ *[646, v]*
▪ qatel ▪ [ˈʔaːtɛl]

steal ▪ *[647, v]*
▪ seraq ▪ /ˈsɛreʔ/

dance ▪ *[648, v]*
▪ żifen ▪ /ˈziːfɛn/

simple ▪ *[659, adj]*
▪ sempliċi ▪

full ▪ *[661, adj]* ▪ *containing maximum*
▪ mimli ▪

small ▪ *[662, adj]*
▪ żgħir ▪ /zaˤjr/

big ▪ *[663, adj]*
▪ kbir ▪ [gbiːr]

narrow ▪ *[669, adj]*
▪ dojoq ▪

wide ▪ *[670, adj]*
▪ wiesgħa ▪ /ˈwiːsa/

black ▪ *[678, adj]*
▪ iswed ▪ /ˈɪswɛt/

grey ▪ *[679, adj]*
▪ griż ▪

white ▪ *[680, adj]*
▪ abjad ▪ /ˈebjet/

blue ▪ *[681, adj]*
▪ ikħal ▪ /ˈɪkħal/

green ▪ *[682, adj]*
▪ aħdar ▪ /ˈeħder/

red ▪ *[683, adj]*
▪ aħmar ▪ /ˈeħmer/

yellow ▪ *[684, adj]*
▪ isfar ▪ /ˈɪsfer/

hot ▪ *[687, adj]* ▪ *temperature*
▪ sħun ▪ /sħʊn/

cold • *[689, adj]*
  • kiesaħ • /ˈkɪːseħ/
hard • *[692, adj]*
  • iebes • /ˈɪːbɛs/
near • *[702, adj]*
  • qrib • /ʔriːp/
weak • *[705, adj]*
  • dgħajjef • /ˈdaˤːjːɛf/
strong • *[706, adj]*
  • qawwi • /ˈʔewːɪ/
clean • *[709, adj]*
  • nadif • /naˈdiːf/
dirty • *[710, adj]*
  • maħmuġ •
past • *[711, adj]*
  • passat • /pasˈsa.t/
present • *[713, adj]*
  • preżent •
new • *[715, adj]*
  • ġdid • /dʒdiːt/
young • *[716, adj]*
  • żagħżugħ • /zaˤːˈzuːħ/
old • *[717, adj]*
  • xiħ • /ʃiːħ/
ancient • *[718, adj]*
  • antik •
historical • *[720, adj]*
  • storiku •
possible • *[722, adj]*
  • possibbli •
dangerous • *[723, adj]*
  • perikolużi •
last • *[732, adj]*
  • l-aħħar •
ill • *[737, adj]*
  • marid • /maˈriːt/
pregnant • *[739, adj]*
  • tqal • /tʔaːl/
hungry • *[740, adj]*
  • bil-ġuħ •
bad • *[753, adj]* • *of evaluation*
  • ħażin • /ħeˈziːn/

important ▪ *[757, adj]*
▪ importanti ▪
ugly ▪ *[764, adj]*
▪ ikrah ▪ /'ɪkrɛħ/
right ▪ *[765, adj]*
▪ korett ▪
easy ▪ *[768, adj]*
▪ faċli ▪ /'fetʃlɪ/
difficult ▪ *[769, adj]*
▪ diffiċli ▪ /dɪ'fːɪtʃlɪ/
good ▪ *[772, adj]* ▪ *of moral*
▪ tajjeb ▪ /'tejːɛp/
brave ▪ *[775, adj]*
▪ kuraġġuż ▪
lazy ▪ *[776, adj]*
▪ għażżien ▪
happy ▪ *[782, adj]*
▪ kuntenti ▪
traditional ▪ *[788, adj]*
▪ tradizzjonali ▪
national ▪ *[789, adj]*
▪ nazzjonali ▪
poor ▪ *[794, adj]*
▪ fqir ▪ /fʔiːr/
cheap ▪ *[795, adj]*
▪ irħis ▪
expensive ▪ *[796, adj]*
▪ għaljin ▪ /al'jiːn/
why ▪ *[797, adv]*
▪ ghaliex ▪
how ▪ *[800, adv]* ▪ *to what degree*
▪ kif ▪
very ▪ *[803, adv]*
▪ ħafna ▪
also ▪ *[808, adv]*
▪ ukoll ▪ /ʊ'kɔll/
down ▪ *[813, adv]*
▪ baxx ▪
there ▪ *[824, adv]* ▪ *place*
▪ hemm ▪ /ɛːmː/
ago ▪ *[827, adv]*
▪ ilu ▪

today ▪ *[830, adv]*
▪ illum ▪
tomorrow ▪ *[832, adv]*
▪ għada ▪ /'aːda/
again ▪ *[837, adv]*
▪ darb' oħra ▪
often ▪ *[838, adv]*
▪ spiss ▪
seldom ▪ *[839, adv]*
▪ rari ▪
soon ▪ *[841, adv]*
▪ dalwaqt ▪
already ▪ *[845, adv]*
▪ diġà ▪
almost ▪ *[846, adv]*
▪ kważi ▪
maybe ▪ *[848, adv]*
▪ forsi ▪ /'fɔrsɪ/
how ▪ *[849, adv]* ▪ *in what manner*
▪ kif ▪
I ▪ *[850, prn]*
▪ jien ▪ /jɪːn/
you ▪ *[853, prn]* ▪ *subject <pl>*
▪ intkom ▪
he ▪ *[854, prn]*
▪ hu ▪
she ▪ *[855, prn]*
▪ hi ▪ /iː/
it ▪ *[856, prn]* ▪ *subjeCT*
▪ hu ▫ <m> ▪ /uː/
▪ hi ▫ <f> ▪ /iː/
they ▪ *[857, prn]*
▪ huma ▪ /'uːmɐ/
everything ▪ *[867, prn]*
▪ kollox ▪ /'kɔllɔʃ/
something ▪ *[869, prn]*
▪ xi ħaġa ▪
what ▪ *[873, prn]*
▪ xiex ▪ /ʃɪːʃ/
who ▪ *[874, prn]*
▪ min ▪
that ▪ *[876, det]*

• dak •

no • *[878, det]*

• xejn •

every • *[879, det]*

• kull •

other • *[882, det]*

• ieħor •

my • *[884, det]*

• tiegħi •

our • *[885, det]*

• tagħna • /ˈtaʕːne/

your • *[886, det]* • *<sg>*

• tiegħek •

your • *[887, det]* • *<pl>*

• tagħkom • /ˈtaʕːkɔm/

his • *[888, det]*

• tiegħu •

her • *[889, det]*

• tagħha • /ˈtaħːa/

their • *[891, det]*

• tagħhom • /ˈtaħːɔm/

which • *[892, det]*

• liema •

more • *[895, det]*

• aktar •

all • *[898, det]*

• kollox • /ˈkɔllɔʃ/

zero • *[899, num]*

• żero •

one • *[900, num]*

• wieħed •
• waħda ▫ <f> •

two • *[901, num]*

• tnejn •

three • *[902, num]*

• tlieta •

four • *[903, num]*

• erbgħa •

five • *[904, num]*

• ħamsa •

six • *[905, num]*

• sitta •

seven ▪ *[906, num]*
▪ sebgħa ▪
eight ▪ *[907, num]*
▪ tmienja ▪
nine ▪ *[908, num]*
▪ disgħa ▪
ten ▪ *[909, num]*
▪ għaxra ▪
eleven ▪ *[910, num]*
▪ ħdax ▪
twelve ▪ *[911, num]*
▪ tnax ▪
thirteen ▪ *[912, num]*
▪ tlettax ▪
fifteen ▪ *[913, num]*
▪ ħmistax ▪
twenty ▪ *[914, num]*
▪ għoxrin ▪
thirty ▪ *[915, num]*
▪ tletin ▪
fifty ▪ *[916, num]*
▪ ħamsin ▪
hundred ▪ *[917, num]*
▪ mija ▪
thousand ▪ *[918, num]*
▪ elf ▪
million ▪ *[919, num]*
▪ miljun ▪
first ▪ *[920, num]*
▪ l-ewwel ▪
second ▪ *[921, num]*
▪ it-tieni ▪
third ▪ *[922, num]*
▪ it-tilet ▪
fifth ▪ *[923, num]*
▪ il-ħames ▪
tenth ▪ *[924, num]*
▪ l-għaxar ▪
and ▪ *[925, cnj]* ▪ *similar words*
▪ u ▪
and ▪ *[926, cnj]* ▪ *last item*
▪ u ▪

122

or • *[927, cnj]*

> • jew • /jɛw/

but • *[928, cnj]*

> • iżda •

that • *[930, cnj]*

> • li •

where • *[934, cnj]*

> • fejn •

because • *[935, cnj]*

> • għaliex • /aˈlɪːʃ/

if • *[937, cnj]* • *supposing that*

> • jekk •

as • *[940, cnj]*

> • kif •

of • *[941, prp]* • *belonging to*

> • ta' • /ta/

of • *[942, prp]* • *containing / made from*

> • ta' • /ta/

for • *[946, prp]* • *because of*

> • għal • /aːl/

for • *[947, prp]* • *intended to*

> • għal • /aːl/

about • *[948, prp]* • *concerning*

> • dwar •

with • *[951, prp]* • *in addition / company*

> • ma' •

without • *[952, prp]*

> • mingħajr • /mɪˈnajr/

from • *[953, prp]* • *with source*

> • minn •

from • *[954, prp]* • *with starting point*

> • minn •

to • *[955, prp]* • *direction*

> • lil •

on • *[966, prp]* • *place*

> • fuq • /fuːʔ/

under • *[968, prp]*

> • taħt • /taħt/

before • *[969, prp]* • *place*

> • quddiem •

between • *[971, prp]*

> • bejn • /bɛjn/

about • *[972, prp]* • *on every side*
- madwar -

at • *[975, prp]* • *time*
- fi -

on • *[976, prp]* • *date*
- fi -

before • *[981, prp]* • *earlier than*
- qabel -

after • *[982, prp]* • *later than*
- wara -

hello • *[983, int]* • *greeting*
- bonġu ▫ {before 12:00 pm} -
- bonswa ▫ {after 12:00 pm} -

hi • *[984, int]*
- ejj -

hello • *[985, int]* • *by telephone*
- ħellow -

welcome • *[986, int]*
- merħba - /'mɛrħbɐ/

goodbye • *[987, int]*
- ċaw -

bye • *[988, int]*
- ċaw -

thanks • *[990, int]*
- grazzi -

you're welcome • *[991, int]*
- m'hemmx għalxiex -

excuse me • *[992, int]*
- skużani -

cheers • *[994, int]*
- saħħa -

happy New Year • *[995, int]*
- Is-Sena t-Tajba -

yes • *[996, int]*
- iva -

no • *[997, int]*
- le -

ABOUT THE LANGUAGES
[ACW] HIJAZI ARABIC
ON THE WIKIPEDIA
https://en.wikipedia.org/wiki/Hijazi_Arabic_language

NAME(S), CODES, TYPE
NAME(S)
- (base) name: Hijazi Arabic
- other name(s): Hejazi Arabic, Hijazi Spoken Arabic

CODES
- code ISO 639-3: acw
- code ISO 639-1: no

TYPE
variety of Arabic macrolanguage [ara/ ar] (living)

SPEAKERS, ETHNIC GROUP(S), REGION(S)
SPEAKERS
- L1: ~11'000'000

ETHNIC GROUP(S)
Arabs

MAIN REGION(S)
- native region(s): Western Asia: Saudi Arabia (Hejaz), United Arab Emirates
- diaspora region(s): no

CLASSIFICATION
Afro-Asiatic > Semitic > Arabic

ACTUAL WRITING SYSTEM(S)
Arabic script (Arabic alphabet)

[ARB] STANDARD ARABIC
ON THE WIKIPEDIA
https://en.wikipedia.org/wiki/Arabic_language

NAME(S), CODES, TYPE
NAME(S)
- (base) name: Standard Arabic
- other name(s): Modern Standard Arabic

CODES
- code ISO 639-3: arb
- code ISO 639-1: no

TYPE
variety of Arabic, mL macrolanguage [ara/ ar] (living)

SPEAKERS, ETHNIC GROUP(S), REGION(S)
SPEAKERS
- L1: no

ETHNIC GROUP(S)
Arabs

MAIN REGION(S)
- native region(s): Western Asia: Saudi Arabia, Bahrain, Iraq, Israel, Jordan, Kuwait, Lebanon, Oman, Palestine, Qatar, Syria, United Arab Emirates, Yemen; Northern Africa: Algeria, Egypt, Libya, Morocco, Sudan, Tunisia; Central Africa: Chad;Western Africa: Mauritania
- diaspora region(s): no

CLASSIFICATION
CLASSIFICATION (SIMPLIFIED)
Afro-Asiatic > Semitic > Arabic

ACTUAL WRITING SYSTEM(S)
Arabic script (Base Arabic alphabet)

[ARY] MOROCCAN ARABIC
ON THE WIKIPEDIA
https://en.wikipedia.org/wiki/Moroccan_Arabic_language

NAME(S), CODES, TYPE
NAME(S)
- (base) name: Moroccan Arabic
- other name(s): Moroccan Spoken Arabic

CODES
- code ISO 639-3: ary
- code ISO 639-1: no

TYPE
variety of Arabic macrolanguage [ara/ ar] (living)

SPEAKERS, ETHNIC GROUP(S), REGION(S)
SPEAKERS
- L1: ~33'000'000

ETHNIC GROUP(S)
Arabs

MAIN REGION(S)
- native region(s): Northern Africa: Morocco
- diaspora region(s): Egypt, Belgium, France, Italy, Netherlands, Spain

CLASSIFICATION
Afro-Asiatic > Semitic > Arabic

ACTUAL WRITING SYSTEM(S)
Arabic script (Arabic alphabet)

[ARZ] EGYPTIAN ARABIC
ON THE WIKIPEDIA
https://en.wikipedia.org/wiki/Egyptian_Arabic_language

NAME(S), CODES, TYPE
NAME(S)
- (base) name: Egyptian Arabic
- other name(s): Egyptian Spoken Arabic, Masri

CODES
- code ISO 639-3: arz
- code ISO 639-1: no

TYPE
variety of Arabic macrolanguage [ara/ ar] (living)

SPEAKERS, ETHNIC GROUP(S), REGION(S)
SPEAKERS
- L1: ~64'000'000

ETHNIC GROUP(S)
Arabs (Egyptians)

MAIN REGION(S)
- native region(s): Northern Africa: Egypt, Libya
- diaspora region(s): Iraq, Kuwait, Saudi Arabia

CLASSIFICATION
Afro-Asiatic > Semitic > Arabic

ACTUAL WRITING SYSTEM(S)
Arabic script (Arabic alphabet)

[MLT] MALTESE
ON THE WIKIPEDIA
https://en.wikipedia.org/wiki/Maltese_language

NAME(S), CODES, TYPE
NAME(S)
- (base) name: Maltese
- other name(s): no

CODES
- code ISO 639-3: mlt
- code ISO 639-1: mt

TYPE
individual language (living)

SPEAKERS, ETHNIC GROUP(S), REGION(S)
SPEAKERS
- L1: ~520'000

ETHNIC GROUP(S)
Maltese people

MAIN REGION(S)
- native region(s): Southwestern Europe: Malta
- diaspora region(s): no

CLASSIFICATION
Afro-Asiatic > Semitic > Arabic

ACTUAL WRITING SYSTEM(S)
Latin script (Maltese alphabet)

ABOUT THE MULTI LINGUIS PROJECT
ABOUT THE PROJECT AND OFFERED DICTIONARIES IN GENERAL

Multi Linguis is an independent indie project. All work on downloading and processing sources, as well as creating books and the website, was carried out by the forces of one person - the author of the project. Although there are other dictionaries of this type, many of the ideas underlying the project are original.

The Multi Linguis Project is based on the corpus of the English version of Wiktionary as well as linguistic articles of Wikipedia and is licensed under the open license Creative Commons CC BY-SA 3.0 (https://creativecommons.org/licenses/by-sa/3.0/deed.en).

The project offers dictionaries for more than 200 languages. These books are bilingual, with translations from the English language into foreign ones.

The Multi Linguis Dictionaries are intended to help you try out different languages, study and compare them, as well as revise the vocabulary. They can be applied separately or as additional tools for the suited educational courses. You may also use them for spelling simple broken phrases, translating and just for fun.

A database of the project includes 9'000 lemmas (that is, morphemes, words and phrases with a specific meaning). This corresponds to levels A1 - B2 by the CEFR (Common European Framework of Reference), or Beginner - Upper Intermediate by other language learning systems. This number covers approximately 100 percent of self-sufficient vocabulary and 85 percent of all word use.

The Multi Linguis Dictionaries are not traditional alphabetical, but frequency-thematic. This means that entries in these books can be arranged by levels, themes, parts of speech or keywords, but never alphabetically. When you use them, you may study often used lemmas previously than rarely used ones, and thematically related groups in unity, rather than separately. In addition, this approach speeds up the process of learning languages, promotes memorization and develops associativity, flexibility and rapidity of lingual thinking.

Several different types, kinds and varieties of dictionaries are offered for the same language. They differ in the number of included lemmas, varieties of the arrangement, the completeness of contained information, external and internal design. To achieve particular purposes, using one option is more effective and convenient than the others.

For all dictionaries of the same type, a universal division into levels, themes, parts of speech and keywords is applied. This means that books of the same type, but different in language have completely equal structure. This approach promotes studying of the second and subsequent foreign languages, as well as comparing them.

The Multi Linguis Dictionaries are available mobile formats (epub and mobi).

In addition to the books, the Multi Linguis Project includes its own website, as well as pages on Facebook and Twitter. We invite you to register there.

ABOUT DESIGN OF DICTIONARIES AND ENTRIES

The Multi Linguis Dictionaries include the following parts - a short description of a title language (languages), descriptions of the project and license, a key to the IPA phonetic symbols and the main part. To make use more convenient, they also contain a table of contents.

The main part consists of a certain number of entries. They are joined into small subsections grouped into larger sections.

The base of the entries are lemmas - dictionary forms of lexemes. A lexeme is a linguistic abstraction that has a specific meaning - grammatical (a role in a sentence) and semantic (subject matter). In speech, lexemes are expressed in the form of particular words or phrases that differ from each other grammatically, graphically and phonologically.

In the entries, lemmas are represented by headers and flags of part of speech. Definitions are not given in the Multi Linguis Project, and therefore their semantic meaning can only be clarified through headlines of the sections. In difficult cases, short tips are offered to facilitate understanding of their meanings.

The entries also contain flags of levels.

The entries contain one or more translations into the title language with indication of its code. In some cases, translations are accompanied by grammatical flags and comments. In addition, entries in the Learner's and Survival Dictionaries can contain transcriptions (IPA characters are used), as well as transliterations for languages with non-Latin scripts.

ABOUT DIVISION OF THE DATABASE INTO LEVELS AND THEMES

Any division into levels and themes given in dictionaries is not indisputable. Structuring of entries is not necessary to create a perfect system (this is impossible) but to make students arrange their own vocabulary. Using proposed division by dictionaries, you will agree or disagree with it, and therefore more effectively build the studied lemmas in the appropriate order to you personally.

Multi Linguis proposes an original division of lemmas into levels, performed as follows:
1. In the Learner's Dictionaries - into 6 so-called learning steps of 1'500 lemmas each: steps 1-2 include the first 3'000 and correspond to levels A1-A2 CEFR, steps 3-4 - the second 3'000 (B1), steps 5-6 - third 3'000 (B2.1-B2.2).
2. In the Survival Dictionaries, there is no division into levels - all lemmas have the same importance (A1 - A2 CEFR).

The levels follow each other in decreasing importance to speakers and frequency of use - that is, the lemmas related to the first one are the most necessary and frequently encountered. Linguistic studies show that the level A1 CEFR covers 10% of self-sufficient vocabulary and 30% of all word use, A1-A2 - 30 and 55, A1-B1 - 60 and 75, A1-B2 - 100 and 85 percent respectively.

Levels are indicated in the entries by special flags.

You may study the Multi Linguis Dictionaries at any convenient speed, and the uniform division used in them will allow you to determine the approximate time that will be spent on each level. For example, at a rate of 5 lemmas per day, it will take as long as 300 days to study a group of 1'500 ones, and at a rate of 50 lemmas per day - only 30.

In addition, Multi Linguis proposes an original division of lemmas into themes:
1. In the Learner's and Survival Dictionaries - into 150 themes.

All themes are joined into 30 super themes and divided into over 2'000 subthemes.

The proposed division describes such vast semantic areas as Properties of objects, Actions, Time, Natural world, Body, Mind, Communication, Society, Economics and others.

Themes and super themes are indicated in the headlines of the sections. Subthemes are indicated only in the Learner's Dictionaries by the alternating gray-white coloring of blocks that include lemmas. There is no indication of themes in the Survival Dictionaries.

Also in the Learner's Dictionaries especially close lemmas are grouped into unbroken sequences to facilitate their studying (for example, North - East - South- West). In this case, the entries, initially referring to different levels by their weights, turn out to be at the same.

ABOUT TYPES AND KINDS OF THE DICTIONARIES

Multi Linguis offers 2 types of dictionaries - Learner's and Survival.

The Learner's Dictionaries can include up to 9'000 lemmas, which are divided into 6 learning steps of 1'500 ones each (corresponding to levels A1 - B2 CEFR), as well as 150 themes grouped into 30 super themes. The entries contain shortened texts of translations from the Wiktionary corpus, and also contain transcriptions.

There are the following kinds of the Learner's dictionaries:

1. For Learning - intended to help you learn all necessary lemmas at once, regardless of their levels. For this, the entries are arranged only by themes.

2. For Learning Step by Step - intended to help you learn necessary lemmas gradually, according to their levels. For this, the entries are arranged by steps and then by themes. This kind is an alternative to the previous one.

3. For Revising - intended to help you revise lemmas in an unusual way. For this, the entries can be arranged by parts of speech or keywords and then by themes.

The Survival Dictionaries are sets of small vocabularies of related languages, which include up to 999 lemmas. These books are intended to help you get a list of elementary lemmas. The entries are arranged by parts of speech and then by themes.

Currently, Multi Linguis is able to create the Learner's Dictionaries for more than 70 languages, and the Survival Dictionaries for more than 200 ones.

ABOUT VARIETIES OF THE ARRANGEMENT OF LEMMAS

Lemmas are complex phenomena that have the following characteristics:

1. Level - shows the importance of a lemma in the vocabulary and approximate frequency of its use;

2. Theme - semantic meaning that it conveys;

3. Part of speech - a grammatical role that it plays in a sentence;

4. Keyword – a group of related words that it belongs to;

5. Rhyme – a group of words with which it is similar in sound or spelling.

The Multi Linguis Dictionaries differ from each other not only in types and range of levels but also in varieties of the arrangement. Entries in them can be arranged by one or two of those characteristics. This is made for you can view the studying language from different angles.

The last (respectively, the second or third) level of arrangement is by parts of speech. It corresponds to gray-white blocks in the Learner's Dictionaries.

ABOUT THE SOURCE, SELECTION OF LEMMAS AND PROCESSING OF ENTRIES

The Multi Linguis Project is based on the Wiktionary corpus, which contains a huge number of English lemmas, their definitions, grammatical and etymological information, as well as translations into many languages and related transcriptions. Wiktionary is maintained by enthusiasts, including native speakers and professional linguists, that makes this source authentic and modern.

At the time of the download, the Wiktionary corpus included approximately 350'000 lemmas, of which approximately 120'000 were translated into at least one language.

Of these, 20'000 lemmas were selected according to their weight. In the Multi Linguis Dictionaries, the main principle of assigning weight is the number of its translations into 80 key languages of the world. Although this approach is an alternative to the standard selection by frequency of use in books, TV programs or spoken speech, it also has the right to exist. Additional principles are the occurrence of the lemma in open frequency lists given on simple.wiktionary.org, as well as the personal opinion of the author of the project about its importance.

Of these, 9'000 lemmas with the highest weight were included in the database of the Learner's Dictionaries, 999 - of the Survival Dictionaries.

For comparison, the total number of lemmas of levels A1-B2 CEFR in professional projects (Cambridge, Oxford, Longman, Macmillan) is approximately 9-10'000.

Levels, themes and keywords were defined for the selected lemmas, also parts of speech were checked and corrected. Morphemes and proper names, as well as unnecessary synonyms, were removed from the databases of the Learner's and Survival Dictionaries.

Related translations and transcriptions from Wiktionary were standardized, errors and typos were corrected whenever possible. They were cut off as close to the beginning as possible, since this is where the most accurate and important varieties of them are located.

ABOUT ERRORS AND CHANGES IN THE SOURCE

Despite strict recommendations for adding new entries, conducting regular rechecks and fighting vandalism, there are still more or less serious errors in the Wiktionary corpus, and therefore in the Multi Linguis database. According to made estimates, the percentage of entries with errors for the corpus of the Russian translations does not exceed 2.5%, and for other languages, the percentage may be slightly higher.

Since the project is carried out by one person, it is likely that errors occurred when processing the source entries. According to made estimates, the percentage of such entries does not exceed 0.5%.

The Wiktionary corpus is constantly updated and supplemented. According to made estimates, the current rate of updating and adding new entries does not exceed 3% per year.

Lemmas and translations for the Multi Linguis Project were downloaded from Wiktionary about 2 years ago, transcriptions - more than a year ago.

ABOUT STORES, PRICES, DISCOUNTS AND PROMOTION

The Multi Linguis Dictionaries are offered for sale in some e-book stores.

The prices of the Multi Linguis Dictionaries do not exceed $8, which is significantly lower than the prices of professional analogues.

The price of a particular dictionary is determined by the range of levels that make it up. The book that includes a wider range has a higher price. You may first buy a small book at a more affordable price to appreciate it and then buy a more voluminous and expensive one.

The price also depends on the completeness of translations of its entries. This means that for books that have at least one of its levels filled with translations of less than 80% (of the Learner's Dictionaries) the prices are reduced by $1. If this rate is lower than 60%, then such books are not created and offered at all. For the Survival Dictionaries, the creation threshold is 333 lemmas. We hope that you will find this approach to price and quality fair.

ABOUT PLANS FOR THE FUTURE AND ADDITIONAL SERVICES

In the future, it is planned to republish the Learner's and Survival Dictionaries. The following updates are outlined: 1. Correction of errors in the database; 2. Increase of the number of translations into various languages; 3. Publication of new dictionaries for both already submitted and novel languages.

It is also possible to be implemented: 1. Redesign of the Learner's and Survival Dictionaries into 3 columns; 2. Publication of the Original Dictionaries (include up to 12'000 lemmas, divided into 4 levels and 300 themes; contain complete translations; include proper names, phrases and morphemes; there are many different types and kinds); 3. Creation of a collection of cards; 4. Creation of a mobile application.

LICENSE INFORMATION

Find detailed information on:
- https://creativecommons.org/licenses/by-sa/3.0/deed.en;
-
https://en.wikipedia.org/wiki/Wikipedia:Text_of_Creative_Commons_At
tribution-ShareAlike_3.0_Unported_License;
- https://creativecommons.org/licenses/by-sa/3.0/legalcode.

The Multi Linguis Project uses only fonts with open licenses:
- Ubuntu (The license is based on the SIL Open Font License);
- Noto (SIL Open Font License);
- Awesome (SIL Open Font License).

Find detailed information on:
- https://scripts.sil.org/cms/scripts/page.php?id=OFL;
- https://en.wikipedia.org/wiki/SIL_Open_Font_License.

Made in the USA
Monee, IL
21 October 2021

80191131R00079